WALKING WITH JESUS TO JERUSALEM

A LENTEN PILGRIMAGE OF HOPE

DIANE AMENTO OWENS

In Memory of
Kali Marie Owens (1988-2017)
who taught us how to be kind and to face
suffering and death with grace and strength

They that hope in the LORD will
   renew their strength,
   they will soar on eagles' wings;
   They will run and not grow weary,
   walk and not grow faint.

— ISAIAH: 40: 31

As disciples of the Lord, we are called to find our greater hope in him, and then, without delay, carry that hope with us, as pilgrims of light amid the darkness of this world.
   — Pope Francis
   December 24, 2024

PROLOGUE

LENT AS A PILGRIMAGE

> We must always be mindful that pilgrimage is an outer journey
> that serves our inner transformation.
> —Christine Valters Painter

Welcome to this Lenten pilgrimage, my fellow traveler. Come along on a journey to accompany Jesus to Jerusalem where the cross awaited him. Each day of our pilgrimage will take us to different locations, including the Holy Land, where we will gaze at sacred images, most of which are crucifixes. Every step of the way, we'll be mindful that this journey will ultimately end in Jerusalem where we will walk with Jesus up the hill to Calvary.

Perhaps you've never thought of Lent as a pilgrimage. I hadn't either until God began nudging me with the pilgrimage theme in 2014 when I read *Jesus: A Pilgrimage* by Fr. James Martin, SJ. Before reading this book, I had no desire to go on a pilgrimage to the Holy Land. But over the next few years, the pilgrimage theme kept popping up in my life and in the lives of people I see for spiritual direction. Then in 2019 I accepted an invitation to join a pilgrimage to the Holy Land.

Prior to this Holy Land pilgrimage, I had been on a different kind of journey with my family, one that I would never have described as a pilgrimage. In January of 2015, my 27-year-old daughter's sudden brain cancer diagnosis sent my family down a road of suffering and uncertainty. Yet every step of the way we were accompanied by the faithful presence of many people and their prayers. In addition to my faith, I relied on several of these same people to steer me, support me, and soothe me with words of comfort and hope. As I look back in my rearview mirror, I clearly see hope present in those faithful people who accompanied us on our own Way of the Cross that ended in Kali's death on April 2, 2017. We were all hoping for an earthly healing for her, but instead God granted my daughter eternal healing.

Kali's death sent me on a sacred journey of immense grief but also one of transformation, especially after I vowed to find meaning in her death. This huge loss has made me more compassionate of others experiencing suffering and loss. Grief cracked my heart open, and compassion poured out of the cracks.

When I began worshipping at a Franciscan church, the San Damiano cross spoke straight to my heart, and shortly before Kali's death I began paying attention to other crucifixes. They were all so different! I felt an unexplainable desire to photograph and gaze at them, and it became my mission to photograph the crucifix in churches everywhere I visited. Yet I had no idea what I was supposed to do with these photos.

On my pilgrimage to the Holy Land the fall of 2019, I collected more photos even though I was trying to travel more as a pilgrim than a tourist. The one photo I did not take was of the heavy cross our tour group carried through the streets of the Old City of Jerusalem, following the path of the Via

Dolorosa. I wore my daughter's purple sweatshirt and needed no photo reminder of the long walk of suffering my family had endured before and after her death. Ultimately, I returned from the pilgrimage transformed by walking where Jesus had walked.

Then the pandemic hit shortly after Ash Wednesday of 2020. I wrote this hopeful entry in my journal:

> What if ashes were not just a sign of death and sin but also the sign of God's promise of bringing new life from the ashes? What if the ashes were seen not so much as a curse but a sign of what's possible, what's been promised to us?

The first few months of the pandemic during Lent and Easter made it hard to look with eyes of hope that see possibility and new life. Mass went online and our lives narrowed to our screens. Gazing at the San Damiano cross in my Franciscan church became my weekly devotion after Sunday distribution of the Eucharist was permitted.

As travel restrictions eased, I became even more mindful of every crucifix I encountered in my travels. I began to wonder: Why do we venerate the cross only during Lent? Why are the Stations of the Cross only a Lenten devotion? The rest of the year we pass by the stations with barely a glance or a prayer. Yet Jesus told us to take up our crosses and follow him. There is always suffering, and the pandemic made our collective crosses more visible.

When Lent 2021 approached, someone I see for spiritual direction asked if I would use my crucifix photo collection to write daily email reflections for her. She knew I like to read reflections, so why not write them? I agreed, knowing that I had enough photos for the forty days of Lent, the Sundays, and the Easter Octave.

When my Lenten writing commitment began, I was several months into another commitment, the Nineteenth Annotation, an eight-month Ignatian retreat in daily life based on the Spiritual Exercises of St. Ignatius. Lent coincided with the part of the retreat focused on the suffering and death of Jesus. While contemplating Matthew's description of Jesus in the Garden of Gethsemane, I wrote this in my prayer journal: "Today, Lord, I ask for the grace to have the courage to accompany you and others on the road of suffering." I realize now that this prayer became one of the themes that would eventually shape this book.

Also during this Lent, as the pandemic continued to isolate and divide us over masking and vaccines, a friend of mine, Fr. Mark Harrington, was hospitalized for six weeks undergoing treatment for a rare cancer that he would eventually succumb to. Whenever I thought of Fr. Mark alone and isolated in his hospital room, it was not a stretch for me to also contemplate the suffering of Jesus.

As for you, my fellow pilgrim, I imagine it's not a stretch to imagine what suffering and loss feel like because you have faced both of these in one way or another. Maybe you've experienced loss of a child through death, addiction, or estrangement. Maybe you've lost a partner through death or divorce. Maybe you've suffered through a sudden job loss or a difficult diagnosis or loss of independence as you've aged. As we travel through these days of Lent together, we'll carry our own heavy crosses of grief, loss, and suffering as we accompany Jesus carrying the immense weight of his. But we will be ever mindful that our journey to Jerusalem is also one of hope—the journey to Jerusalem led to death AND new life!

The prophet Isaiah tells us that "by his wounds we were healed." (Isaiah 53:5) As you gaze upon the wounds of the crucified Jesus each of these days of Lent, may your reflection, prayer, and actions draw you closer to the One Who Suffered because he loved us. May these days lead you on a pilgrimage of healing from your sorrows and losses, your sufferings and pain, your shame—all the wounds that are part of being human. As Fr. Greg Boyle, SJ, writes in *Tattoos on the Heart*: "No part of our hardwiring or our messy selves is to be disparaged. Where we stand, in all our mistakes and imperfections, is holy ground." May Jesus meet us there!

PREPARE FOR YOUR LENTEN PILGRIMAGE

Lent is a journey of *return to God*. How many times, in our activity or indifference, have we told him: 'Lord, I will come to you later, just wait a little. . . I can't come today, but tomorrow I will begin to pray and do something for others.' We do this, time and time again. Right now, however, God is speaking to our hearts. In this life, we will always have things to do and excuses to offer, but right now, brothers and sisters, right now is the time to return to God.
　—Pope Francis, February 2, 2017

Unlike a special pilgrimage, Lent comes around every year. Do you sometimes feel like it sneaks up on you? If Lent begins especially early, it seems like we've barely put away our Christmas spirits and bright lights—and putting on sackcloth and ashes isn't exactly something to look forward to. This year, consider entering into Lent not like a dreaded time but more like a pilgrimage, a sacred time set aside to grow closer to Jesus and the cross he embraced. And like any pilgrimage, preparation is key.

Before Lent begins, reflect on your goal for this Lent. Is your desire to grow closer to Jesus by spending more time with him? Perhaps you desire to become more like Jesus—more loving, humble, or nonjudgmental. If you've chosen this book as your Lenten companion, I hope that the photos, reflections, prayers, and suggestions for daily practice will be a helpful guide.

You may be familiar with Lectio Divina, "Sacred Reading," but you may want to try a prayer practice called Visio Divina, "Sacred Seeing," to contemplate one of this book's many images. You'll find instructions for both practices in the resource section.

Please note that the cited Scripture passages for each reflection are not necessarily from that day's Lectionary reading; this enables these reflections to apply during any cycle of the liturgical year. However, the Sunday passages are taken from Cycle B, and the Easter Octave passages from John appear in all three liturgical cycles.

As Pope Francis reminds us, each Lent is an opportunity to return to God. Growing in relationship with Jesus is the best way I know how to do this. Who is Jesus for you? As you walk with him this Lent, watch what he does, see what he sees, love what he loves. Allow Jesus to speak to your heart. And at the end of this sacred Lenten pilgrimage, may you be ready to meet the Risen Jesus.

And your ears shall hear a word behind you:

"This is the way; walk in it,"
When you would turn to the right or the left.
—Isaiah: 30: 21

For Your Reflection:
Who are you today and who would you like to be after you have walked this road with Jesus?

ASH WEDNESDAY

Behold, now is a very acceptable time; behold, now is the day of salvation. 2 Corinthians 6:2

Mission San Xavier del Bac; Tucson, Arizona

On the altar of this old mission church, front and center is a life-sized statue in priestly vestments. Perhaps it's St. Francis Xavier for whom the mission is named or Jesuit missionary Fr. Kino who laid the foundation for the mission in 1700. Dwarfed by the statue and in between large, scantily clothed cherubs,

Jesus hangs, crucified. His cross rises out of a large pyramid-shaped block of wood almost half the size of the crucifix. There is a lot going on, and the small crucifix appears insignificant compared to everything else.

On a side altar, a wooden figure lay at rest partly enclosed by glass. Somewhat out of curiosity after Mass, I join the line of people inching along to venerate the wooden image. Eventually I am close enough to read the sign, "Please do not come to visit St. Francis during Mass." Because of the line's length, I understand the sign's wisdom. Clearly the parishioners of the mission have a strong devotion and connection to St. Francis Xavier. But what about their devotion to Jesus? Why weren't people also lined up to venerate the crucifix like we do every year on Good Friday?

I can question the faith of Mission San Xavier's parishioners and the many tourists and pilgrims who journey into the Arizona desert to visit this shrine. But what importance does the cross of Jesus play in *my* life, and do I really notice it, contemplate it, or pray before it? If this is the centerpiece of my faith, how often do I place it front and center in my life? Am I willing to follow Jesus all the way to Jerusalem and Calvary?

The first day of Lent is a good day to ponder these questions.

PRAYER

My Jesus, you hung for three hours on a piece of wood—insignificant, ignored, rejected, and humiliated. Your cross is the ultimate symbol of your surrender to the will of your Father. Help me to accept the hardships, the suffering, and the sorrows in my life—some days are so hard! Be with me when I want to give up. Help me to remember that you, Jesus, and only you, are the center of my life. Grant me the grace to see your presence clearly in the midst of all the things that distract me from you today and during each of these forty days of Lent.

REFLECT & RESPOND

As Lent begins, spend some time gazing at a crucifix and pondering what you need to do to place Jesus front and center in your life. Choose one thing to do and begin today. And you will have at least forty more days to practice this one thing!

THURSDAY AFTER ASH WEDNESDAY

He summoned the crowd with his disciples and said to them, "Whoever wishes to come after me must deny himself, take up his cross, and follow me." Mark 8:34

St. Patrick Catholic Community Chapel; Scottsdale, Arizona

As Lent begins, I sit and gaze at the crucifix behind this chapel's altar. Until today I've always focused on the outstretched arms of Jesus, gathering me in, inviting me into his embrace. But all I can focus on today is the enormity of the cross. It overpowers the golden body of Jesus. Its wooden shape ends in four large wooden boxes, the points of the cross. Today, I am overwhelmed by the power of the cross to overtake Jesus and the power of my cross to overtake me.

For three hours Jesus hung on this instrument of torture and pain, and for those three hours it must have seemed like the cross—like death—would win. And then for three days it seemed as if death had indeed won. But this overwhelmingly large cross led to life. Can I look past the cross and see it not as an instrument of suffering but as a testament to love?

The more I look at the huge wooden cross dwarfing the body of Jesus, the more I wonder about the artist who designed this particular crucifix. What message did he or she have for me? And suddenly I see the cross with new eyes. The four boxes "box in" or define a smaller cross—a cross proportional to the body of Jesus. The boxes are like an artistic decoration, and now my eyes can see only Jesus and his small cross.

When I look at my life and the cross I'm meant to carry, what do I see? Do I focus on the small daily sufferings—the times of letting go, the disappointments, the frustrations? Or do I look at my enormous loss? The overwhelming suffering while walking with my daughter through brain cancer and then her eventual death—a loss that seemed unimaginable and far too heavy for one to carry or even bear for a moment. And where *was* Jesus in the middle of my cross? My loss is as huge and disproportionate to my idea of what it means to have a "good and fair life" as is this image hanging before me.

But in the middle is Jesus. Hanging there. Suffering then, and mindful of my suffering now. He *is* inviting me to him after all. "Come and I will be with you," he says. "Don't hide your face from my suffering or your own. We will carry this; we will bear this together."

I realize that my suffering has nothing to do with being good or fair or undeserving. Nor did the suffering of Jesus on the cross. My suffering just is and is a consequence of being human. But the suffering of Jesus had a purpose. St. Ignatius said that love is shown more in deeds than in words. On the wall before me I see love in action. A mighty deed. And a visible sign that suffering and death lead to new life.

"Come," the arms of Jesus beckon, "I will lead you to new life. I will lead you home. I will lead you through fear and darkness to light and life. Take up your cross and follow me. You'll see what I have prepared for you."

PRAYER

Oh Jesus, my fear seems much bigger than my faith. Give me eyes to see you in the darkness of grief and loss. Reach out your hand as a daily reminder that you are always with me. Through pain and sorrow. Through tears and laughter. Through longing and emptiness. In moments of joy and incredible lightness of being. Let the anxiety and uncertainty of my fear be reminders of what you endured, you, the lamb led to slaughter. Draw me closer to you this Lent, through the wood of your cross. Keep my eyes fixed on you and your suffering as I bear my own. Be my companion, O Shepherd on the Cross. I want to walk this journey with you.

REFLECT & RESPOND

What's one concrete thing you can do today to put love into action? Small acts are just as important as large, highly visible actions, just as long as you actually *do* them.

FRIDAY AFTER ASH WEDNESDAY

For whoever wishes to save his life will lose it, but whoever loses his life for my sake will save it. Luke 9:24

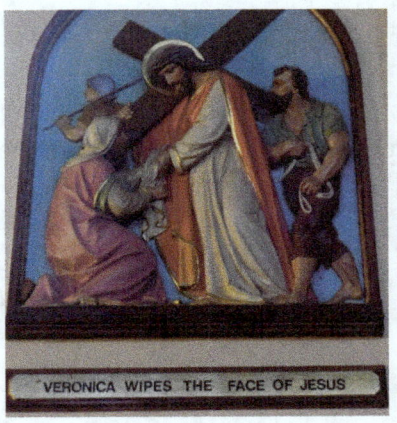

St. Mary of the Visitation Catholic Church; Iowa City, Iowa

The vivid colors of this station of the cross nestled between two stained glass windows stop me during my visit to this old church, and I think of that day when Veronica stopped to help Jesus as he was carrying his heavy cross through the streets of

Jerusalem. Although the garments of Jesus and Veronica are brightly colored, there is no visible blood anywhere on Jesus. But I know that Veronica was paying attention to his suffering that day, and she stopped to offer him a cloth to wipe off his hot, blood-streaked face.

She didn't just watch him walk by, hanging her head in sorrow. She *did* something. A small act of love. Even if it seemed that her action would not be enough to alleviate his pain and suffering. I imagine myself as an onlooker in the crowd using Ignatian contemplation. As if I were an eyewitness of this scene, I observe Veronica and her compassionate act of love, and this is what I write in my journal:

> She extends the white cloth, and she wipes his face. As he hands it back to her, he looks into her eyes and she into his. Through his parched and bleeding lips, he says, "Thank you." After Jesus passed by, her eyes fill with tears. She feels so useless witnessing this gentle man suffer so visibly. It didn't seem like her act of kindness was enough, but it was all she had to offer. She realizes she is still clutching the white cloth and smooths it out onto her lap. The outline of Jesus's face looks back at her. Perhaps it was enough after all.

PRAYER

Dear Jesus, help me to be like Veronica and to pay attention to the needs of others in distress. Give me the courage to stop to help someone who is suffering. I want to be like Veronica and offer a small act of love, of care. When I see tears streaming down the face of another, I don't want to just stand there, feeling useless and helpless. May I offer a loving touch or a kind word. Guide me so that I may be fully present to another's pain and to know that sometimes the gift of my presence is enough.

Choose one person today to be deliberately present to, no matter what they are experiencing. Make your presence feel like a small act of caring for them.

SATURDAY AFTER ASH WEDNESDAY

I gave my back to those who beat me; my cheeks to those who tore out my beard; my face I did not hide from insults and spitting. Isaiah 50:6

Creighton University Retreat Center; Griswold, Iowa

This sculptured corpus in the chapel is a crucifix like nothing I've ever seen! From a distance, it almost looks like the body of Jesus has some sort of skin disorder. But as I get closer, I see clearly that each "bump" is the face of someone.

I sit for a while in the presence of this crucifix and reflect on this most unique image that so visually represents the meaning of crucifixion:

I see your people, Lord, and I see your downward gaze as you look upon them in your suffering and in theirs. You have no face—just the face of others, so I cannot see your sadness and your pain, but I can see it in the faces of your people covering you like skin.

Your sweet sorrowful head is hung low in pain and from the weight of all of us you're thinking about and dying for. And you thought of me. I am humbled. I am grateful. I am loved beyond measure.

Your arms uphold the sufferings of millions—how can I learn to reach out to your people like you did on the cross?

Your outstretched hands say two different things—your left hand says, "I do this for you, I do this for your glory, Father." Your right hand seems to say, "Here, *you* do this in memory of me. You. Here, I leave you in charge."

Your right foot is placed somewhat ahead of your left. Another message: "Do this. Go here. Follow me into the arms of the hopeless and the lonely and the grieved."

PRAYER

Jesus, you hung on the cross weighed down by our often cruel faces and hearts of stone. You became one of us to share in our humanity, and you died under the weight of our sins. May I see your face reflected in everyone I meet, but especially in the sad and lonely people whom I encounter, either on a street corner or in my own life. May I have the courage to reach out and accompany them in their need. Open my eyes, Lord, so that I may see your face everywhere I go.

REFLECT & RESPOND

Our faces can convey a lot of good will to other people. Today whenever you see a familiar face or the checkout clerk or a stranger, greet them with your smile.

FIRST SUNDAY OF LENT

And he remained in the desert for forty days, tempted by Satan. He was among wild beasts, and the angels ministered to him. Mark 1:12-15

In *Tattoos on the Heart,* Fr. Greg Boyle, SJ, tells the story of former gang member Alex, a "homie" whom Fr. Greg describes as having a heart true and pure. "Blessed are the single-hearted," Fr. Greg writes. "Jesus meant Alex."

Later, Alex has an encounter with a flight attendant at 34,000 feet and explains to her what life is like at Homeboy Industries, the gang intervention program Fr. Greg founded in Los Angeles. She cries when Alex relates that he was one of three gang members who had just been invited to dinner at the White House. Fr. Greg assures Alex that her reaction was to be expected. "She just caught a glimpse of ya. She saw that you are somebody. She recognized you . . . as the shape of God's heart."

What is the shape of God's heart?

Some people may believe that God's heart is not all loving—that God's heart doesn't have tender, ruffled edges. But Jesus came to show us the heart of God, and the heart of Jesus was gentle, inclusive, and compassionate.

In today's gospel from Mark, Jesus went out to the desert to be alone without distractions. We tend to focus on the temptations from the Evil One on this first Sunday of Lent. But what about the angels? I'm pretty sure that when the angels ministered to Jesus fasting in the desert, his heart was expanding as he grew into the acceptance that he was indeed the Beloved Son of God. I imagine his heart becoming in sync with the heart of God the Father.

Perhaps a worthy goal for Lent is to focus on our hearts. To shape them, reshape them, widen them, open them, soften them . . . The list goes on. I personally want to reshape my heart to be more like the heart of Jesus. What about you?

> We need to ask for the grace to have a heart like the heart of God—one made in the likeness of God that feels pain when witnessing others suffer.
> —Pope Francis, Homily,
> February 19, 2019

FIRST WEEK OF LENT

Pilgrimages invite us to ponder
the deeper questions of life:
Why are we are here?
Where are we headed?
How do we get there?

—J. Michael Sparough, SJ; "Pilgrimage,"
a post on the Ignatian Spirituality website

MONDAY, FIRST WEEK OF LENT

When he returned he found them asleep. He said to Peter, "Simon, are you asleep? Could you not keep watch for one hour?" Mark 14:37

Chapel of St. Francis, Prudential Center; Boston, Massachusetts

This small chapel, tucked into a corner of a busy Boston shopping mall, seems out of place across from a restaurant bustling with the lunch crowd. Perhaps the space had been a store before it was converted into this sanctuary of peace and prayer.

The noontime Mass is celebrated underneath the San

Damiano cross, the same crucifix that hangs over the altar at my home parish. It's the same cross that St. Francis was praying before when he heard God tell him to rebuild his church. The San Damiano cross always reminds me to look beyond suffering and death to Resurrection. This cross tells a story—even Peter's crowing rooster is represented. The cross does not represent the end of my story and yours, but only the beginning: Jesus is represented as tortured *and* triumphant.

During every Mass—whether your church is located in a shopping mall or live-streamed from afar—Jesus beckons: "The table is set. Come, dine with me. Come and be fed with my body. Come away from your busy lives—your shopping, your work, your fast-food. Come and eat from the banquet I've prepared for you. Please don't eat and run—that's not good manners, is it?"

Following Mass, the Blessed Sacrament is exposed on the altar. Should I remain or leave for lunch? Should I pause to remember the two great acts of love, Eucharist and Crucifixion, displayed in front of me?

As I gaze upon the cross that once spoke to St. Francis, I write this message in my journal:

Stay with me. Remain here with me. Watch and pray.
Don't go to sleep in my presence. Don't turn your back
on me. I know what awaits me: death on a cross preceded
by horrendous torture. I will be condemned to die—for
what? So until my hour is at hand, stay with me.

I choose to stay a while. Every act of devotion and presence is a conscious choice. And when I do leave this place, the world offers daily opportunities to be fully present to the suffering of those I encounter.

PRAYER

Dear Jesus, feed me with your presence. I hunger for you. I hunger for silence. I need your presence in all the business and busyness of my life. Draw me closer, Lord. Calm my restlessness and my doing-ness that often amounts to nothing-ness. I want to sit at your feet and listen. Speak, Lord, your servant is listening. I will be still and know that you are God.

REFLECT & RESPOND

Today, despite the busyness of your life, choose to make a deliberate effort to gaze at a crucifix in your home or at church and share with Jesus what you see.

TUESDAY, FIRST WEEK OF LENT

Jesus answered and said to them, "Destroy this temple and in three days I will raise it up." John 2: 19

Phoenix Jesuit Morning of Reflection; Marriott Conference Center

I notice the small crucifix on the altar as the priest walks behind it to begin Mass. Barely 10 inches tall, the cross sits atop the banquet-size hotel tablecloth covering the altar. The priest's leather-covered Bible is the only other prop on the altar as he begins Mass during our Lenten morning of reflection.

Noticing the crucifix is a normal observation for me, but this one is different. Usually a crucifix is a permanent and prominent fixture behind the altar. Yet this miniature and moveable symbol is barely noticeable, and after Mass begins, the small cross blends into the background.

I don't look up at the crucifix throughout the homily as the priest reflects on the word "up" and its significance in today's gospel when Jesus talked about "raising it up," referring to the temple of his body. The priest concludes his homily by suggesting other ways during Lent that we might reflect on action words combined with "up."

I don't look up and notice the little crucifix as I pass directly in front of it to receive the Eucharist. But after I return to my seat, suddenly the cross seems to be lit up like a beacon as I sing the words to the old hymn, "One Bread, One Body." I fix my eyes on the tiny symbol of love and suffering—a sacred body in brass on a wooden cross—as I remember the long ago act of love for me, for you, for all of us. "We are one body in this one Lord."

One small crucifix indeed, but look, just look up at such great love and sacrifice!

PRAYER

Jesus, may your cross and what it represents be my focus during this season of Lent. I know that we your followers are all broken people but oh-so-loved. I could measure the size of this tiny crucifix, but no one could ever be able to measure the love you displayed on it. Can I even dare to measure up to the extravagant love you have for me—the same love you have for every single person? May I have the courage to empty myself as you did, to be your body, to unite my heart with yours, and multiply your act of love. Ultimately, Jesus, may I be willing to follow you up to Jerusalem and all the way up the hill to Calvary.

REFLECT & RESPOND

How many times today can you look **UP** from your phone and refocus your attention on something that is more life giving?

WEDNESDAY THE FIRST WEEK
OF LENT

He said to them, "Why are you sleeping? Get up and pray that you may not undergo the test." Luke 22:46

Chapel of the Holy Cross; Sedona, Arizona

Rejected. Alone Jesus hangs on the twisted limbs of the tree. His body is contorted in suffering, and his open eyes look downward at me—at everyone who put him on this cross.

The view of Sedona's red rocks through the huge window behind the crucifix is breathtaking. Yet, the suffering of the crucified man before me reminds me that suffering still exists in every corner of our world. Can I see both the beauty and the suffering, or do I turn away from signs of suffering around me? Where am I supposed to place my attention?

As I sit gazing at the twisted tree and the bent body of Jesus, a young woman walks up the three steps of the altar, turns, and poses. Right in front of this vivid image of torture, she smiles as her male companion captures the moment. And still you hang there, Jesus, in extreme suffering and rejection, the backdrop for a happy photo memory of the Chapel of the Holy Cross. It's as if many of us are asleep, unaware of your suffering—or the suffering of others.

One week of Lent has passed, and I struggle to enter into the pain and suffering of Jesus. To accompany him as he walks the steps that inevitably led to Jerusalem and Calvary. And I struggle to be the voice of hope for those around me who are grieving or struggling with difficult situations. What can I do to accompany them? I'd rather focus my attention on happy social media posts and photos. I want to turn away from all the suffering in the world.

Suddenly I realize I am no different from the woman posing for a photo, her back to the crucifix. With a deep sigh, I refocus on this season of Lent. I need to turn around and look at Jesus suffering on the cross. I need to focus on changing my sinful ways, and I must place my attention on becoming more like Jesus.

I seek silence and solitude. I gaze at Jesus crucified on a twisted cross. I contemplate his heart of pure and endless love. I listen for where I am to place my attention and what I am to do out of love. I ask for the grace to stay awake and be aware of whatever God calls me to do during the rest of these forty days.

PRAYER

Lord, give me eyes to see your broken body in the world. Give me the heart of compassion to recognize you in the suffering faces of those I meet. Help me to minister to the wounds of the broken. Show me the way to accompany your suffering people and to be a sign of hope for them. During these forty days, Jesus, show me the way to make my heart more like yours.

REFLECT & RESPOND

A good question to reflect on during your silent prayer is: Who are you calling me to notice today, Lord? Ask for the awareness to notice at least one person around you today who needs your kind attention.

THURSDAY OF THE FIRST WEEK
OF LENT

He humbled himself, becoming obedient to death, even death on a cross. Philippians 2:8

St. Patrick Catholic Community Chapel; Scottsdale, Arizona

Every time I serve as sacristan and lector for Mass, I pass by this crucifix atop a pole. It leans against a darkened corner in a passageway from the sacristy to the Daily Mass Chapel. Behind the scenes. Most days I barely notice its presence.

Today, however, I notice that the artist designed this crucifix differently from most others I observe. Rather than hanging his head down to his right, this Jesus bows his head downward. The words "in humble surrender" come to mind. His head is bowed in acceptance, in respect, in servitude. His eyes are cast downward in a silent "yes." He stretches out his arms in love, in forgiveness, in a gesture both empowered and powerless.

What might I learn from you, Jesus, in your act of humility and self-emptying love? How might I learn to endure and accept what your Father gives me? How can I stretch out my arms, my hands, and wait for what—I know not what—the uncertainty of the future? As you hung on the cross, you knew your certainty was death. But were you comforted—or could you even comprehend—that in three days your Father would "raise up" this temple of you?

May I be comforted in knowing that the very worst thing I ever endured—my daughter's cancer diagnosis and two years of suffering—ultimately led to her journey home to your Father's arms. Your head may be bowed in humble surrender to death, O Lord, but death is never the end of your story or mine.

PRAYER

Oh, Jesus, when I want to despair and give up hope, help me to bow my head to the Father's will, knowing that he always has my best interests in mind, even though I cannot imagine the future. Be with those who are facing the last moments of their earthly pilgrimage today. May they feel your presence in their final hours. May they hear whispered words of comfort from those who love them. And may they fly from the arms of loved ones to your outstretched arms of welcome that say, "Yes, my child, you are home."

REFLECT & RESPOND

How does pride lead you to act like you don't need God? Today, pray for the grace of humility and then humble yourself by asking someone for help—even if it's help for something small. Asking for help and feeling vulnerable is often hard, so it's best to begin slowly.

FRIDAY OF THE FIRST WEEK
OF LENT

Great crowds came to him, having with them the lame, the blind, the deformed, the mute, and many others. They placed them at his feet, and he cured them. Matthew 15:30

Meditation Chapel, Franciscan Renewal Center; Scottsdale, Arizona

On the way to the meditation chapel, I notice a single brown leaf covered with tiny beads of water. Even in its brown and wrinkled state, the leaf is still beautiful and useful, still giving God glory by reflecting the light in its small drops. It is open. Available. Accepting. It wouldn't have been able catch these drops if it had been curled up, near death. How interesting that I stop to notice this single leaf. That I stop to marvel at its beauty. I realize with a smile that this little leaf is a reminder of the focus word I have chosen for the year: *open*.

Upon entering the small meditation chapel, I wonder how I can be more open. As I gaze at this small San Damiano crucifix next to a stunning stained glass window, I see this image of crucified Jesus in an entirely new light:

Christ's arms are open.
Christ's hands are open.
Christ's feet are open.
Christ's eyes are open.
Christ's love is open for all.
Christ is open to the Spirit descending on him like a
dove.
Christ will always be open to the will of his Father.

Then I reflect on the many colors of the stained glass window and the symbol of the Holy Spirit. I think of the openness to creativity that the creators of the window and this San Damiano cross must have had. My eyes wander to a stained glass lamp near the window, and I am surprised to see an image of a leaf in the same shape as the one I had admired outside.

Coincidence? Perhaps. But I've learned that when we are awake and open to what's on the path before us, we receive so much more of what God wants to give us. I recall the words of Fr. Jim Martin, SJ, as he ends every Examen podcast: "Just keep noticing!"

Yes, I will. Will you join me in noticing what God places on each of our paths today?

PRAYER

Lord, help me to see you in every fallen leaf. In those fallen examples of humanity that you place on my path every day.

Help me to see you glorified in the broken, the dried-up, the old, and the discarded. Help me to be open to receive the blessing of those who are lit from within by your light. Most of all, O Light of the World, help me to be open to those opportunities to carry your light of love to those I meet today.

REFLECT & RESPOND

Today, make an effort to slow down so that you are able to notice those who appear on your path and are in need of your love and acceptance. None of us will ever be the great healer that Jesus was, but by paying attention to someone else's needs you can provide a healing balm in ways you may not fully appreciate.

SATURDAY OF THE FIRST WEEK OF LENT

Then Jesus told his disciples, "Whoever wishes to come after me, must deny himself, take up his cross, and follow me." Matthew 16: 24-25

Kafr Kanna (Cana); North District, Israel

At the site of Christ's first miracle at the wedding feast at Cana, I study this depiction of the seventh station, Jesus falling a second time under the weight of his cross. I recall how Jesus changed water into wine after Mary told the servants at the wedding feast, "Do whatever he tells you." In this crucifixion scene, Jesus is in no shape to be working any miracles.

I think of the disciples who had either watched this sad event unfolding from a safe distance or hid in fear that they'd be crucified next. I think of Mary who had witnessed her son's first miracle and now *this*.

Jesus had told his disciples, "Take up your cross." At the time did they think, "Lord, you want us to do *what*? Haven't we already given up enough to follow you?" As their master and teacher was sold for thirty pieces of silver, did they remember what Jesus told them about taking up their cross? Did they finally understand what he meant? If only Mary had been able to remind these friends of Jesus to "do whatever he tells you." But now she carried her own heavy cross as she witnessed her son carrying his, stumbling and suffering through the streets of Jerusalem.

And what does it mean to me when I hear, "Take up your cross"? I have lived under the weight of a cross while watching my daughter suffer and die, and I still live under that cross, four years after her death. But if I look around, it doesn't take long to notice others struggling under the weight of their physical or emotional burdens. Fr. Greg Boyle, SJ, describes in *Tattoos on the Heart* standing in awe at the pain others carry "dumbstruck by the sheer size of the burden—more than I've ever been asked to carry."

Carrying the heavy cross of cancer and loss and grief has widened my heart. I know that I am meant to use what happened to me to accompany others. If I simply show up with a caring heart, I hope I am able to lighten the burden of another, just by my presence. A heavy cross is not meant to be carried alone.

PRAYER

Jesus, help guide me to my own path of discipleship. Grant me the grace so that I may use the many gifts you have given me to serve others. Give me the strength to bear the weight of my own crosses and help others to bear theirs. Speak to my heart, dear Jesus, and widen it to become more like yours.

REFLECT & RESPOND

Today, practice being a generous listener to someone else's story. Don't try to fix their situation or give them unwanted advice or tell them about a time you faced something similar. Just listen. Be present, and be as compassionate as Jesus was with people who were suffering.

SECOND SUNDAY OF LENT

He [Peter] hardly knew what to say, they were so terrified. Mark 9:2-10

Pilgrims like me who want to reach the top of Mount Tabor in Israel ride a rickety tour bus up a twisty, curvy road. After our bus reaches the top, I wonder how the three trusted disciples Peter, James, and John felt after they ascended this mountain on foot with Jesus. I imagine that they all needed a long rest. Still, they followed their master up the mountain, and the scripture passage says that Jesus led them up there "apart, by themselves." Did he want to get away from the crowds? Was there a reason he took only these three? And why climb this particular mountain?

At some point after their ascent, the three disciples witnessed a strange and awe-inspiring scene unfold. They were justifiably terrified, and the scripture passage says that Peter "did not know what to say." Yet he had just made a proposal to make three dwellings to honor Elijah, Moses, and Jesus.

In spite of his terror, Peter was making plans. His mind was spinning. But what was his heart telling him?

No doubt the three disciples were even more terrified when the cloud enveloped Jesus and his companions, and God announced that Jesus is his beloved Son and said, "Listen to him!"

Today's reading reminds us that sometimes you must simply be present to God—no plans, no attestations, no words needed. We don't even have to go to a mountaintop to do this. But our minds—our continuous stream of thoughts—often prevent us from entering into stillness where we can listen to Jesus speak to our hearts.

This dazzling moment on Mount Tabor did not require planning and action. This bright white vision required presence and quiet contemplation.

How can I enter into stillness today so that Jesus is able to speak to my heart?

We are afraid of moments of silence. Let us not be afraid! It will do us good. And the benefit to our hearts will also heal our tongue, our words, and above all our choices.
—Pope Francis, General Audience,
December 15, 2021

SECOND WEEK OF LENT

The beginning of the path to finding God is awareness. Not simply awareness of the ways that you can find God, but an awareness that God desires to find you.

—James Martin, SJ; *The Jesuit Guide to (Almost) Everything: A Spirituality for Real Life*

MONDAY OF THE SECOND WEEK OF LENT

He took the child by the hand and said to her, "Talitha koum," which means, "Little girl, I say to you, arise!" Mark 5:41

St. Patrick Church; Council Bluffs, Iowa

On a visit to my hometown, I stop by my childhood parish church that had been torn down, relocated, and rebuilt. A kind woman whom I met in the restroom volunteers to give me an unofficial tour after I tell her I am a former parishioner.

When we enter the sanctuary, I gasp as soon as I notice the ornate stations of the cross lining the walls. My tour guide confirms that these are indeed the stations from the old church. After the tour, I choose this station to photograph.

Later while sorting through my photos, I realize that this particular station reminds me of my Holy Land pilgrimage when I attended Mass at the Church of the Holy Sepulchre. I was selected to proclaim the first reading just a few feet away from the tomb. Afterward we stood in a long line waiting our turn to spend a moment in the tomb's small space. Prompted by an observation of Fr. James Martin, SJ, in *Jesus: A Pilgrimage*, I was mindful that the tomb was not only a place for death and burial but was also the place of the Resurrection.

This station reminds me of what it must have been like for Mary to look at the face of her dead son, saying goodbye and believing she would never see him again. I think of the others with her at the tomb caring for his body to prepare it for burial, their sorrow as heavy as the stone they placed Jesus on. None of them knew what would happen on the third day, even though Jesus had spoken of it a few times. Did they even have an inkling then that dying had to come before rising? Had any of them dared to hope even the size of a sliver that he would rise up from this cold and dark tomb, walk into the light, and walk back into their lives?

PRAYER

Lord Jesus, I know you restore people to life. Moved by compassion, you restored to life the daughter of Jairus and the son of the widow of Nain. Restore me, Jesus, to wholeness and to freedom so that I may serve in your kingdom. Strengthen my confidence and embolden me to move in directions that are difficult, especially in accompanying those who are suffering.

Help me, Jesus. Grasp my hand and tell me, "Rise up and be on your way!"

REFLECT & RESPOND

Who is someone you know who has experienced the recent loss of someone dear to them? Stop and pray for this person who is grieving. Then go one step further and reach out (via text, a phone call, or a greeting card) to let them know you're thinking about them and the dear one they've lost.

TUESDAY OF THE SECOND WEEK
OF LENT

Come to me, all you who labor and are burdened, and I will give you rest. Matthew 11:28

Our Lady of the Angels Church; Scottsdale, Arizona

I sit in the empty church and gaze up at the San Damiano cross. I think of St. Francis of Assisi who received a message while he was gazing at this same crucifix so long ago. "Rebuild my church," God told Francis. I sit and pray and gaze. I do not receive a clear message like St. Francis did, but it is the image itself that whispers to my heart. I continue to focus on the outstretched arms of Jesus that seem to be a gesture of invitation as I imagine him speaking to me. I write in my journal what I hear in my heart:

> Here I am. Come. Bring me your burdens and your own
> crosses that are too heavy to bear, and I will help you
> carry them. Lean on me. Today. For I am Emmanuel. I
> am God with you. These outstretched fingers are
> reaching for you, the same way they did when I was a
> tiny baby in my mother's arms. I want to wrap my fingers
> around your heart. I want you to feel held by me,
> depending on me for your every need. Give me your
> heart as I have given you mine. Here. Now.
> Come to me. I am waiting at your door.
> Come, open the door of your heart to me.
> Come. I bring the light that fills your darkness.
> Come. I carry a lantern of love to warm your weary
> spirit.
> I am waiting and knocking ever so gently. Invite me in.
> Open your arms and your life to me.
> I'm longing to hear you whisper: 'Come, Lord Jesus. Be
> with me. Remain with me.'
> Place your hand in mine and trust me. Today and always.

PRAYER

My Jesus, thank you for the gift of faith. Help my unbelief on those days when my spirit is dim and weak . . . on those days when I cannot hear you calling me. Open my ears so I hear your loving invitation. Open my eyes to notice your outstretched hands. Open my heart to your ever-present and faithful love. Yes, you are Emmanuel, God with me, in all your forms, whether you are a tiny baby or a dying man on a cross. Come, Lord Jesus, come.

REFLECT & RESPOND

Today, imagine Jesus inviting you to spend ten minutes gazing at a crucifix in your home, in a book or online, or in a church. As you sit in silence, pay attention to the thoughts and feelings that rise within you as you look at this sacred image. If you have a journal, you may want to take some extra time to write about what you have experienced and heard during your gazing time. For extra guidance, refer to the description of Visio Divina that appears in the resource section at the end of this book.

WEDNESDAY OF THE SECOND
WEEK OF LENT

The dead man came out, tied hand and foot with burial bands, and his face was wrapped in a cloth. Jesus said to them, "Untie him, and let him go." John 11:44

Creighton Retreat Center; Griswold, Iowa

I remember the day I had chosen this laminated Celtic cross, a familiar symbol I had selected from the many scattered on a table at a retreat. When I returned to my seat and read the message on the back, I immediately wanted to choose a different cross. Why hadn't my cross contained the kind of message others received like "Create" or "Receive"? I can do both of those really well!

Let go. Why has this always been so hard for me? But this particular cross with its message was apparently what I needed on that day, just six months after my daughter's death. And today as I stare again at the laminated cross's message, I realize "let go" is what I especially need this Lent as I prepare to let go of my daughter's car that I inherited from her.

Today, memories come flooding back of driving her to her radiation treatments. The seizures she had experienced prohibited her from driving, so I was her more-than-willing chauffeur. How she loved that car! And how she hated not being able to drive it because of "dumb cancer."

Today, I will let go of her beloved car. Today, I will see for the last time the "Be Kind" bumper sticker that I had put on the car as a remembrance of my daughter's sweet nature. And today will be the last chance I might hear the phantom sound the radio sometimes makes when the car starts. The startling noise is a reminder that my daughter's spirit is with me—highly amused, no doubt—and I smile as I remember the sound of her laughter.

I know that God speaks to us through memories. The late, great Catholic writer Brian Doyle (who also passed away from brain cancer a few months after my daughter) wrote, "Time stutters and reverses and it is always yesterday and today. Maybe the greatest miracle is memory." Today, I am oh-so-grateful for precious memories. The car will be driven away, but the memories of my sweet daughter are planted in my heart. I refuse to let go of them.

PRAYER

Lord, thank you for the gift of memories. Thank you, Jesus, for leaving us special memories of your time on earth in all the scripture passages that remind us of who you are. We can no longer see you, but we know how much you love us. May we be comforted by precious memories of those we have lost. May we be comforted with the knowledge that our loved ones have their home with you. And may we believe without a doubt that one day we shall be reunited with them. May we live like people of hope.

REFLECT & RESPOND

Be grateful today for a possession you have that used to belong to someone else. Hold it if you can or touch it. Savor your memories of this person, whether living or dead. Is the possession itself more meaningful or is it the memories? How easy would it be to let go of this possession?

THURSDAY OF THE
SECOND WEEK

I have the strength for everything through him who empowers me.
Philippians 4:13

St. Patrick Church; Carlsbad, California

Measly. That's the first thing I think of as I look at this stone-carved crucifix. Really, the arms of Jesus were that puny and weak? How am I supposed to depend on Him when weakness is all I see on this crucifix? Suddenly, I see the humanity of Jesus as I gaze at this cross. And humanity is weak and vulnerable and marked by inescapable suffering. This Jesus, this broken body that hung on the cross, could not escape death, his ultimate act of solidarity with us humans. But this death would lead to his resurrected life. Transformed. Changed. Glorious. Alive, yet bearing the wounds he suffered.

So yes, when I look at this crucifix, I see his physical weakness and his inability to save himself as he surrendered to the will of the Father and succumbed to death.

Unlike Jesus, I resist surrendering to the will of the Father. I want to be in control—I *think* I am in control—but it is God who is in control. I am puny and weak. I am vulnerable and not in control. I hurt. And I thirst. Just like Jesus.

So do not see my puny arms, Jesus tells me. See my humanity and know that I understand what you're going through in your moments of weakness and despair and sorrow. Puny arms or not, I will carry you through your suffering. Believe in the Resurrection. Live with that hope in your heart.

PRAYER

Lord, when I am weak, you are strong. When I feel no hope, I need only to look at your cross and know that death is never the end of the story. Light does come from the darkest dark. If I focus my eyes on your cross, I cannot help but look beyond the cross and see Resurrection, your risen glorified body—no more puny arms or messy humanity. Carry me, Jesus.

REFLECT & RESPOND

What is one weakness you have that helps you to realize your need for God? Reflect on how this weakness affects your relationship with God, and humbly ask God to help you become a better human in spite of this weakness. Today, forgive others for their weaknesses.

FRIDAY OF THE SECOND WEEK OF LENT

He got into the boat with them and the wind died down. They were completely astounded. Mark 6:51

La Casa de Maria Retreat Center; Santa Barbara, California

In 2018 I downloaded this photo from social media that was taken at a retreat center I had previously visited. I cannot recall being inside this chapel, but when I see this photo, the devastation from a mudslide a few days earlier takes my breath away.

Above the destruction, there is Jesus hanging on the cross.

Jesus, whose head is hung even lower than on most crucifixes I photograph. Jesus, whose broken body hangs in rejection, in abandonment. Jesus, whose very life seemed at this point to mirror the devastating scene below the crucifix. This chapel's destruction may seem hopeless, but slowly the restoration process continues.

What we have all experienced from COVID-19 seems like a massive mudslide that affected every single person on this earth. During this tragic time, our "mud-covered" eyes were unable to see our future clearly or with any certainty, and the fear of disease and death was ever present.

Yet no matter what, Jesus is always present. When we suffer, he suffers. He knows what it was like to suffer persecution and death. While he walked on this earth during his public ministry, he reached out to those he encountered who were suffering and mourning.

Jesus can always be found in our suffering somewhere—stuck in the muck with us. He offers restoration in the midst of our worst destruction. And he's always reaching out his hand to quiet our storms. When he was walking on the water during a storm at sea, he told his disciples, "Take courage, it is I, do not be afraid!" (Mark 6:50) Then he got into the boat with them and the wind died down. Why not welcome Jesus into the boat with you?

PRAYER

My Jesus, help me to feel your presence when life is hard. When suffering seems like utter destruction and I cannot see any way out of the mud, allow me to hear your voice of encouragement and hope. Help me to always look up at you when I'm caught in the muck of fear and misfortune—the image of you hanging on your cross always assures me that I am never alone. You endured such horrible suffering! Yet your cross will always remind me that death is not the end of the story.

REFLECT & RESPOND

Is there someone you know whose life is especially messy and mucky? Reach out to them today, knowing you won't be able to fix their mess. Instead focus on bringing a little light to them as a sign of hope.

SATURDAY OF THE SECOND
WEEK OF LENT

Jesus spoke to them again saying, "I am the light of the world. Whoever follows me will not walk in darkness, but will have the light of life." John 8:12

St. Wenceslaus Church; Iowa City, Iowa

The intricate carvings on this beautiful crucifix catch my eye, from the details of the crown of thorns Jesus wears down to the nail heads poking out from his hands and the tops of his feet. The artist portrays the arms of Jesus straight out, and his feet seem to rest gently on the wooden platform beneath them. In wood, the face of Jesus looks almost at rest, as if he is already dead.

As I gaze at this cross, I notice the start of preparations for Saturday afternoon Mass. A priest carrying a very tall ladder appears on the altar then disappears behind a 10-foot high wall next to the altar upon which an angel statue rests. Soon the priest's face pops up above the wall as his arm lifts a candle lighter to the angel's lamp. He repeats the lamp lighting on the opposite side of the altar and then carries off the ladder. I am in awe of this feat—I don't do ladders, and even short stepladders sometimes give me pause because of my fear of heights. After Mass, the same priest would likely be the one who would twice climb the tall ladder and snuff out the two lamps. How can he do this so easily?

As I leave the church, the priest happens to be standing near the door. "Father, I'm so impressed by all you do to light the angel's lamp!"

He dismisses what I think of as a courageous act. "It's no big deal for me. I was a gymnast in college, and I got used to doing things like this."

I walk away from the church, pondering what he told me. What do I do for you, Jesus, that's no big deal for me? What skills and talents have you given me to use in building your kingdom? I think of this church's crucifix artist who was given the talent to create a lasting work that people can use to meditate on how much love Jesus had for us. Not everyone can climb heights or create out of wood, but we can all do something, however small it may seem to us.

PRAYER

Lord, sometimes I feel like I don't do enough to serve you. Sometimes I feel like I'm more focused on what I cannot do than on what I can. I want to be your light in the world. Jesus, how might I light the way for you with my gifts? Send me your Holy Spirit to guide me as I discern how to use my gifts. Help me to be bold in climbing up all those "ladders" I'm afraid to tackle. Give me your grace to do even small things for you and to be more like St. Teresa of Calcutta who reminds us to do small things with great love.

REFLECT & RESPOND

Consider one skill or ability that comes easily for you that you could offer in service to someone else. Use this "no big deal" ability today to make one small offering for someone else's benefit. If the person comments about your offering, humbly accept their gratitude and resist saying that "it's no big deal."

THIRD SUNDAY OF LENT

But Jesus did not need anyone to testify about human nature. He himself understood it well. John 2:13-25

Many consider this Gospel of Jesus driving out the merchants and moneychangers from the temple as proof that he was fully human. Indeed it clearly shows his anger at those who had made his Father's house into a marketplace. The passage states that his disciples' reaction is to recall the words of Scripture (Psalm 69), "Zeal for your house will consume me."

The word "zeal" is not a word commonly used today. It's defined as "great energy or enthusiasm in pursuit of a cause or an objective; eagerness and ardent interest in pursuit of something." Today we may even use the word "passionate" to describe Jesus and some of the things he did.

However you describe the actions of Jesus that day in the temple, it seems that he is showing us a way of being. When we see something that's wrong, we should speak up. Get a little angry if need be. If we are to be followers of Jesus, we need to watch what Jesus does, go where he goes, and do what he does. We too need to be consumed with the things that consumed

Jesus. In this passage from the Gospel of John, he is consumed with anger over the greed and hypocrisy he sees. When Jesus fed the five thousand, all four gospels tell the story of when his compassion for the hungry crowd consumed him, and he multiplied five loaves and two fish to care for their needs. But always, always at the heart of what Jesus was about was doing the will of his Father.

What consumes me this Lent and how can I clear out my own temple to make room for Jesus? Note: You'll want to contemplate two different meanings of "consume." One is "to engage fully." Another is "to use up or squander."

> Let us walk in the world as Jesus did, and let us make our whole existence a sign of our love for our brothers, especially the weakest and poorest; let us build for God a temple of our lives.
> —Pope Francis, Homily, Third Sunday of Lent
> March 15, 2008

THIRD WEEK OF LENT

Even a trip across town to a favorite church or cemetery can become a mini-pilgrimage. It's the prayerful intention that transforms a mere trip into a pilgrimage. Pilgrims hold a holy intention before their hearts, so each step of the journey is an opportunity to ponder life's deeper mysteries.

—J. Michael Sparough, SJ; "Pilgrimage," a post on the Ignatian Spirituality website

MONDAY OF THE THIRD WEEK OF LENT

And you, Bethlehem, land of Judah, are by no means least among the rulers of Judah; since from you shall come a ruler who is to shepherd my people Israel. Matthew 2:6

St. Jerome's Cave, Church of the Nativity; Bethlehem, Palestine

Recently I overheard a woman tell a friend she and her husband planned a trip to have "something to look forward to." When life is hard, we all need something to look forward to.

For Jesus, his final journey to Jerusalem was certainly not something he eagerly anticipated. Throughout the gospels, he often referenced "going up to Jerusalem," but he did not use pleasant details to describe the journey. In Mark 10:33-34, he tells the disciples that he will be "handed over to the chief priests and the scribes and they will condemn him to death and hand him over to the Gentiles who will mock him, spit upon him, scourge him, and put him to death . . ." Jesus knew *exactly* what awaited him, but he went to Jerusalem anyway!

This small crucifix hangs on the wall in a chapel referred to as St. Jerome's Cave, located underneath the Church of the Nativity. It is one of the first things I photograph as I begin my 2019 Holy Land pilgrimage in Bethlehem.

Here in Bethlehem, this tiny and almost insignificant image hangs next to a carved-into-the-wall Chi-Rho, the ancient symbol for Christ.

Here in the City of David, the journey of Jesus to Jerusalem and the cross began when his mother laid his tiny body in a wooden manger, a feeding trough for animals. Thirty-three years later in her son's short earthly life, she stood at the base of a cruciform piece of wood that held her dying son's body. From the manger to the cross: surely her journey as a mother was not what she imagined it would be.

Here in the little town of Bethlehem, the body of Jesus hangs on a twisted cross, and the dark iron of his body does not reveal many details. The only noticeable difference this crucifix has over others I have photographed is that the arms of Jesus are bent, perhaps depicting his effort to lift himself up so that he could breathe. This one detail is a reminder that crucifixion was a horrible way to die.

Jesus, I cannot begin to imagine the pain and suffering of your passion and death. Everyone except your mother and the beloved disciple ran away in fear. Would I too have run away, Jesus? Help me to imitate the faithfulness of your mother and the beloved disciple who stayed with you until the end. Help me to think of them when I want to avoid the suffering of another. Give me the strength to face another's wounds or sorrows and not turn my back. When I'd rather run away, give me the courage to accompany others on difficult journeys.

REFLECT & RESPOND

Take one aspect of the crucifixion (such as the crown of thorns, the nails driven through the hands and feet of Jesus) and try to imagine how much pain Jesus underwent, perhaps by remembering how painful an injury of yours was. After you have reflected on the pain Jesus endured, meditate on the phrase, "Look at what love did for me."

TUESDAY OF THE THIRD WEEK OF LENT

And as he watched Jesus walk by, he exclaimed, "Behold the Lamb of God!" John 1:36

St. John Francis Regis Chapel, Regis University; Denver, Colorado

This chapel is large enough to be an actual church, and from where I sit to the right of the altar, a low-hanging section of the ceiling almost completely obscures my view of the crucifix above the altar. Christ's left hand is all I see. "You must be my hands," I hear Jesus tell me throughout Mass.

The priest's homily from January of 2017 about the baptism of Jesus remains with me. He says that at the time of Jesus, "lamb" was another word for children. He tells us that the Lamb of God was God's term of endearment for his beloved son, like we'd say with pride "my sweet child" or "that's my kid." Later in Mass, when the priest says, "This is the Lamb of God," as he holds up the Eucharist, I feel the statement's impact—the closeness of Jesus as the Son of God, his blessedness and specialness, the love and pride of the Father for his son.

At Communion time, I leave the side seating area to walk down the center aisle toward the altar. I almost gasp out loud when I look up and see this crucifix. Jesus looks so real in his porcelain body that my first thought is, "He looks just like one of us!" Indeed.

After Mass, I am compelled to go back into the chapel to photograph this crucifix. I didn't know it at the time, but I would soon begin my journey carrying my heaviest cross—the one that was meant just for me—my walk through suffering and sorrow, my path through grief and grace. One week later would be the beginning of the end of my daughter's struggle after the discovery of a third recurrence of her brain cancer. My kid. My favored one. My sweet lamb would suffer and die.

But I do know now that Jesus has walked every step of that journey with me. And I have been blessed by so many others who have been his hands reaching out to minister to *me*. Christ's human hands remain on earth through the work of hands like yours and mine. We are called to be the helping hands of hope for others.

PRAYER

Lamb of God, have mercy on us. Lamb of God, use me—my hands, my feet, my voice, all my gifts that you have so freely given me. I am at your service for the Kingdom. I will help to build your kingdom here on earth. I will minister to your people who are carrying their own crosses. Walk with me, gentle Jesus, and show me the way.

REFLECT & RESPOND

Today, be on the lookout for someone who needs help. Make a purposeful effort to use either your hands or your feet in service to this person in need.

WEDNESDAY OF THE THIRD
WEEK OF LENT

A clean heart create for me, God; renew within me a steadfast spirit.
Psalm 51:12

St. Cecilia Parish; Boston, Massachusetts

I enter through the heavy doors of this old red-brick church for quiet prayer, but before I get very far, this crucifix in the narthex stops me. Am I supposed to admire this cross for its ornate artistry like the Israelites must have done with their golden calf? Am I supposed to notice the beautiful imagery on the cross—the lavish designs, the sunburst halo—but ignore the crucified body of Jesus? What did the artist intend for me to to focus on?

The longer I gaze at this image, I suddenly find myself in silent conversation with Jesus:

> I cannot hear your cries and your groans, Jesus. I cannot see the blood dripping down, the inhumanity of this act against you, the horror. I can only see your head thrown back, contorted in your suffering. Your eyes are closed in agony. But they are also closed in surrender, in acceptance.
>
> And those who did this to you, Jesus? They looked at you with coldness and mockery. What kind of person pounds nails into another's hands? What kind of people yell out, "Crucify him! Crucify him!"? Your living, breathing human body underwent such pain!
>
> Then I think: I too, Jesus. I too have crucified you when I've turned my back on the poor or the marginalized. I too have pounded in nails when I speak harsh words. I too have gone along with the crowd even when I knew it was not the right thing to do. My cold and hardened heart continues to keep you on this cross.

PRAYER

Dear Lord, this beautiful, artistic cross cannot detract from your suffering. Your eyes look out at me and at others—all of us who you are hanging on this cross for. Show me how to love others whose appearance is unappealing or distasteful, and to see beyond their exterior and, better yet, try to see them like you do, Jesus. Transform my faith into something real—not the kind of faith to show off like a golden image, but a faith I feel in my heart and live out loud. Show me what's important, Lord. Transform my heart.

REFLECT & RESPOND

Take special care today to speak loving, kind words to everyone you encounter, especially family members who may annoy you or try your patience.

THURSDAY OF THE THIRD WEEK
OF LENT

Even though I walk through the valley of the shadow of death, I will
fear no evil, for you are with me; your rod and your staff comfort me.
Psalm 23:4

St. John's Church, Creighton University; Omaha, Nebraska

On a mid-October Sunday, I climb the concrete steps of this
Omaha landmark to attend Mass here for the first time.

Suddenly I get a little misty-eyed as I imagine my parents standing at the top of these steps in October of 1949 after saying their vows to one another at the altar inside. This is where my story began, I think. I walk inside the old church, and immediately my eyes are drawn to the cross suspended above the altar.

Someone later tells me that because of its design and position, this is known as a rood cross. Regardless of its name or position, I cannot keep my eyes off this unusual crucifix and the two people standing on a crossbar at its base. It looks like a 3D version of the twelfth station of the cross depicting the death of Jesus as his mother and the beloved disciple keep watch. From where I'm sitting, I imagine that it's two *women* who accompany Jesus in his last moments of suffering.

Women ministering to others. I recall all the women who accompanied me after my daughter's cancer was first diagnosed, during the two hopeful years of her treatment, on the weekend of her death, and during the days and weeks that followed. Whether these women were faithful prayer warriors or showed up in person or via email or text, I never felt abandoned or alone. These women were visible signs of God's presence as I walked my own journey of the cross. Just like the two who accompanied Jesus at the base of this rood cross, the women witnessed my suffering, my discouragement, my fear, my hope, and my sorrow. Their simple presence was sometimes all I needed. They were the rod and staff from the Twenty-third Psalm that I visualized I could lean on. And lean on them I did.

I am grateful for every single one of them who walked the path with me. Surely you too can think of people who have stood by you in difficult times. Think of them now as you look at this cross and say a prayer of gratitude.

PRAYER

Dear Jesus, it is not easy to accompany someone I love when they face difficulties, but somehow by your grace I still manage to show up. Grant me the faithfulness of your mother and your beloved disciple so that I may stand with others in their suffering. Being with others who are in pain is really hard, Jesus, and I would rather not enter into their suffering. Give me the courage, compassion, and faithfulness so that I may be present to others in their time of need. Please help me to be okay with my powerlessness in those situations that I cannot fix or change, and to be like your faithful mother and disciple who stood powerless at the foot or your cross.

REFLECT & RESPOND

Ponder the suffering of someone you know and reach out to them in encouragement. This can be as simple as sending a text to say you're thinking of them or praying for them. Today, you may be their only visible sign of God's presence. You may be their light in the darkness, their rod and staff to lean on. You may be just the spark of hope that they need to get through this day.

FRIDAY OF THE THIRD WEEK
OF LENT

See what love the Father has bestowed on us that we may be called the children of God. Yet so we are. 1 John 3:1

Priory of the Church of the Holy Cross, Crosier Village; Phoenix, Arizona

After praying noon prayers with the Crosiers in their lovely little chapel, I had to photograph this unusual cross, the first

Hispanic crucifix I have come across. Yet it is the perfect image for this chapel and the ministry of the Crosier priests to the Hispanic population of South Phoenix.

Jesus once asked his disciples, "Who do you say that I am?" Many of us tend to think of Jesus in terms of the human features that we are most familiar with. I remember my childhood Jesus had blue eyes like me, and I probably held on to some of those early images until my visit to the Holy Land. A Middle-Eastern Jesus looks nothing like me.

Perhaps it's more important to focus on what Jesus *did* rather than what he looked like. He didn't exclude people or avoid the excluded. He dined with Zacchaeus the tax collector. He spoke to a Samaritan woman and asked her for a drink of water. He didn't turn his back on lepers.

So who do I say that you are, Jesus? How can I imitate what you did when you walked among us?

The Crosier priests and brothers understand who Jesus was and that's who they try to be like. Their mission: they touch suffering with hope, they walk with those in need, and they pray with you and for you. Many of those they minister to in South Phoenix probably do resemble the Jesus figure on this rough-hewn, simple crucifix. Being able to relate to Jesus as someone who is "just like us" can strengthen our relationship with God who meets us where we are.

Who do I say that you are, Jesus? And how can I follow what you do?

PRAYER

Loving God, you have created us each in your own image, yet we are all so different! Help me to respect those differences and to be open to so-called outsiders, just like your Son Jesus did when he encountered the Samaritan woman at the well.

Remove the barriers that separate us and help us to see one another as brothers and sisters.

REFLECT & RESPOND

Be especially aware of differences you notice in those around you today. Can you look beyond the differences of other people and remember they are all part of God's family, just like you? Try to see others through the loving eyes of Jesus. If you find their differences bothersome, say to yourself, "This person is just like me." Then look for similarities.

SATURDAY OF THE THIRD WEEK
OF LENT

So whoever is in Christ is a new creation: the old things have passed away; behold, new things have come. 2 Corinthians 5:17

Boston Public Library, Copley Square; Boston, Massachusetts

While perusing my crucifix photo album, I come upon this startling image from 2017 that I didn't remember seeing or photographing. I trace the photo from my camera's location feature and discover my eyes had been drawn to an ornate crucifix in a metropolitan public library.

Research revealed that this image was part of a mural series,

Triumph of Religion, by John Singer Sargent. The artist chose to paint key moments in the history of the Judeo-Christian religion, a mural he worked on for twenty-nine years until his sudden death in 1925. He was unable to finish his final panel, the Sermon on the Mount.

Today as I gaze at this crucifix surrounded by kings above and angels below, I reflect on the artist and his passion to create. It is astonishing that he spent so many years on this particular project. Begun in his studio in England, this massive project was transported in four phases to Boston, four journeys that Sargent personally made with his precious work. As for that last project, did he have any warning that he would not complete it?

Sargent's grand mural series inspires me to keep going day after day, year after year, in service of my work to build God's Kingdom on earth. The artist's work reminds me to concentrate on my purpose. And his unfinished mural panel reminds me of the prayer attributed to St. Oscar Romero (actually written by Bishop Ken Untener), part of which is:

> The Kingdom is not only beyond our efforts, it is even
> beyond our vision. We accomplish in our lifetime only a
> tiny fraction of the magnificent enterprise that is God's
> work. Nothing we do is complete, which is a way of
> saying that the Kingdom always lies beyond us . . . This
> enables us to do something, and to do it very well. It may
> be incomplete, but it is a beginning, a step along the way,
> an opportunity for the Lord's grace to enter and do the
> rest.

PRAYER

Lord Jesus, allow your grace to enter me and do what I cannot do alone. Give me the grace to be persistent and to follow through on the work that is mine to do. In the words of St.

Ignatius, "Give me only your love and your grace. That is enough for me."

REFLECT & RESPOND

Asking the question, "What is mine to do?" is especially helpful when we are tempted to "fix" other people, give unwanted advice, or try to help someone who really needs to do their own work. Carry this question in your back pocket today and act accordingly.

FOURTH SUNDAY OF LENT

But whoever lives the truth comes to the light, so that his works may be clearly seen as done in God. John 3:14-21

For this fourth Sunday of Lent, many parishes use John's Gospel about the man born blind if they will welcome new members into the Catholic church at the Easter Vigil. Today's alternate gospel passage begins just after Jesus meets Nicodemus, a Pharisee and "a ruler of the Jews." Nicodemus appears only in John's Gospel and comes to Jesus at night to question him about his identity. This particular passage, which contains only Jesus's responses to Nicodemus, includes one of the most quoted passages of the Bible, John 3:16: "For God so loved the world that he gave his only Son, so that everyone who believes in him might not perish but might have eternal life."

Nicodemus reminds me of Zacchaeus who climbed a tree so that he could see who Jesus was. Yet unlike Zacchaeus, Nicodemus comes to Jesus in the darkness of night. A Jewish leader like Nicodemus needed to be careful about wanting to know more about Jesus. What was driving this Pharisee's curiosity? Was he disillusioned with the faith of his ancestors?

Yet he couldn't risk his reputation—at least not yet—so under the cover of night, he brings his questions to the teacher.

Clearly there was something about Jesus that attracted Nicodemus to him. Even though Nicodemus arrived in darkness, he moved toward the light of Jesus. And clearly Jesus had an influence on him. Together with Joseph of Arimathea, another secret follower of Jesus, Nicodemus showed up with spices to anoint the body of Jesus after his death. The darkness of death and fear of the Jewish leaders did not keep him away.

Like Nicodemus, do I long to learn more about Jesus and who he was? Am I sometimes afraid to live my faith out loud and in the light?

Whoever seeks the truth, that is, who practices what is good, comes to the light, illuminates the paths of life. Whoever walks in the light, whoever approaches the light, cannot but do good works. This is what we are called to do with greater dedication during Lent: to welcome the light into our conscience, to open our hearts to God's infinite love, to his mercy full of tenderness and goodness, to his forgiveness.

—Pope Francis, Homily, Fourth Sunday of Lent
    March 21, 2014

FOURTH WEEK OF LENT

The true pilgrim is the one who has no need to capture every piece of beauty. I'm always a bit envious as I see them sitting quietly receiving the beauty instead of trying to capture it. They pray with the lens of their eyes and their hearts. They are able to gaze upon, to reverence and adore. They serve as wondrous models for those of us who find it easier to clutch, to possess, to collect.

—Macrina Wiederkehr, OSB; *Seasons of Your Heart*

MONDAY OF THE FOURTH WEEK OF LENT

The angel said to her in reply, "The Holy Spirit will come upon you, and the power of the Most High will overshadow you. Therefore the child to be born will be called holy, the Son of God. Luke 1:35

St. Patrick Catholic Church; Iowa City, Iowa

During the 2018 Advent season, I hadn't been able to stop looking at this crucifix suspended over the altar of this modern church. Below the crucifix on either side is a mural of many saints with their eyes looking upward, just like my upward gaze. With so many holy distractions, how does one focus on what the priest is doing on the altar below?

I also focused my gaze on the painting of the dove behind the crucifix, recalling the role of the Spirit at the Annunciation. Surely it was the Spirit who had "overshadowed" the rebuilding of this magnificent church after the previous building sustained heavy tornado damage on Holy Thursday a decade ago. Renewal is indeed the work of the Spirit, and through the power of the Holy Spirit, God continues to make "everything new," transforming and "rebuilding" *us*.

During this Lenten season, this photo takes me back to the day I sat in awe of this beautiful worship space and the breathtakingly realistic crucifix. I notice that the artist portrayed the nails as having been placed just below Jesus's wrists rather than into the palms of his hands. Either way, I cannot imagine the excruciating pain Jesus endured while the nails were being pounded into his flesh—no matter where the nails went.

As I gaze at this crucifix, I think of the song one of my daughters recently sent me, "God, Turn It Around." I modify the words:

> God, you turned around
> this twisted, damaged old church.
> God, you turned around
> this crucified and broken body.
> God, turn me around.

PRAYER

God, I'm not sure that I am undergoing the kind of change you wish for me this Lent. I get so easily distracted and off track! Holy Spirit, come and overshadow me. Turn me around this

Lent and draw me closer to you, God. Turn me around and change me into a more loving person. Turn me around and change my unkind judgments of people into kind and loving thoughts. Jesus, turn me around and make me more like you.

REFLECT & RESPOND

What is one distraction that prevents you from focusing more of your attention on Jesus this Lent? It's not too late to work on changing your focus. You may find it helpful to ask the Holy Spirit to overshadow your life and help you change what needs to be changed.

TUESDAY OF THE FOURTH WEEK
OF LENT

When they had finished breakfast, Jesus said to Simon Peter, "Simon, son of John, do you love me more than these?" He said to him, "Yes, Lord, you know that I love you." He said to him, "Feed my lambs." John 21:15

Assisted Living Facility; Scottsdale, Arizona

This may seem like a strange photo among all the other crucifixes depicting the suffering Jesus. It actually surprised me when I saw it in my photo album because I didn't remember taking this picture. But I know exactly where I was, and it was not a church. This crucifix of the Risen Christ, the white cloth underneath it, and the gold ciborium were all part of my setup for a Communion service I held for residents of an assisted living facility. I usually serve at a different facility, but this Sunday I was standing in for another Communion minister.

Before I begin the service, I introduce myself and try to learn a few of the residents' names. When I see this photo of the Risen Jesus crucifix, I know for sure it was Anita who handed me her unique cross to use that day.

This photo reminds me of the many years I ministered to the elderly, many of whom became quite dear to me. Just thinking of some of the people I met through this ministry makes me smile. Many faces flash before me; many died during the course of my ministry. Just last week, I was given the gift of what St. Ignatius calls a consoling memory: an especially sweet woman and her obvious delight in seeing me literally popped into my mind. "I knew it would be you today!" she had told me while I was spending time with her after the Communion service. Sometimes I was not sure who was ministering to whom.

But this Risen Jesus crucifix reminds me that once a month for many years I faithfully brought the Body of Christ—the Risen Jesus!—to this special group of people. I offered myself and my time to them, and it never felt like a duty or a chore. Such a privilege to bring Jesus to them, to feed "his lambs."

PRAYER

Jesus, you told Peter to feed your lambs and tend your sheep. I want to be your follower and serve your people. May you continue to sustain the elderly in their loneliness and isolation. Open my heart to those you want me to serve—whoever they are—and help me not to hold back in fear or to let my excuses get in the way. Send me, Lord.

REFLECT & RESPOND

Today practice the ministry of the everyday. Is there a lonely or elderly person you can reach out to or spend time with? Don't forget to look within your own family. It really doesn't require a lot of time to make another person feel seen and special.

WEDNESDAY OF THE FOURTH
WEEK OF LENT

For the foolishness of God is wiser than human wisdom, and the weakness of God is stronger than human strength. 1 Corinthians 1:25

Sacred Heart Church; Coronado, California

I made it a point on vacation to stop by this church to see their crucifix. It probably didn't make a big impression on me at the time—I was simply a woman on a photography mission back then. Now I look at this crucifix and think: this is what courage looks like; however, I realize that vulnerability and powerlessness are what many people may think when they look at a man hanging helplessly on a cross. I recall that the word "courage" comes from the Latin word for "heart." This crucifix represents the courage of Jesus who was willing to be crucified because he had a heart bursting wide open in love.

There are six candles placed on a long table underneath this bronze cross, and two porcelain angels at each end of the table are turned toward Jesus, their hands outstretched as if to say, "Behold."

Who or what do I "glorify"? Where am I directing two angels and six candlesticks' worth of my focus and attention? Is it toward Jesus, the suffering servant, or toward things of this world that provide only temporary happiness?

It is a good question to ponder, especially during this Lent when God desires my heart to turn in his direction.

PRAYER

Jesus, it's hard for me to imagine the kind of love you had that you willingly allowed yourself to be arrested, tortured, and crucified. Behold your sacred heart. Make my heart more like yours: more available to others, more kind and generous, more focused on doing the will of the Father.

REFLECT & RESPOND

Today, focus on the practice of "generous availability" throughout your entire day. Be willing to be generous with your time and your attention.

THURSDAY OF THE FOURTH
WEEK OF LENT

Jesus told her [Martha], "I am the resurrection and the life; whoever believes in me even if he dies, will live. And everyone who lives and believes in me will never die. Do you believe this?" She said to him, "Yes, Lord. I have come to believe that you are the Messiah, the Son of God, the one who is coming into the world." John 11:26-27

St. Bridget Catholic Church; Mesa, Arizona

I slip into this church after a meeting and am greeted by this ghostly green crucifix suspended high above the altar. Rather than reflect on this eerie lighting the day after St. Patrick's Day,

I center my attention on two things: the position of Jesus's arms and the INRI sign.

A few years ago psychologist Amy Cuddy proposed her idea of "power posing." One of these poses involved standing with your arms in a V-position. I actually tried standing this way in a restroom stall before giving a few presentations, but I'm not sure if this stance made me feel any more powerful or confident. However, I see Jesus's arms spread in the same V-position —obviously not a position he chose to be in. But those who put him on the cross asserted their power over this gentle Messiah from Nazareth. They assumed that placing Jesus in this position would end his powerful reign over his kingdom. They were wrong. And could they have ever imagined that his "power pose" on the cross stood for V for victory over death?

The tilted and crooked sign "INRI" represents the words "Jesus of Nazareth, King of the Jews," which according to John's Gospel were written in Hebrew, Latin, and Greek. The sign was a cruel and final mockery of Jesus. The problem is that no matter what the Jewish leaders believed about Jesus, he *was* who he said he was! The position of the sign on this crucifix reminds me that not all that I believe is true. Some of my beliefs may be downright slanted.

What do I actually believe about Jesus? At Mass, we say the words of the Nicene Creed or the Apostles Creed. How often do I think of what those words actually mean? If Jesus stood before me as he did to Martha in the opening Scripture passage and he asked, "Do you believe this?" would I be able to answer like Martha did?

PRAYER

Sometimes I find it hard to believe that you love me exactly the way I am, Jesus. Help my unbelief. Show me how to love the way you do. As hard as it sometimes is to believe that this

96

instrument of death represents love, help me to understand the kind of powerful love you poured out on me from the cross.

REFLECT & RESPOND

What do you believe about Jesus? Today write down your own list of what you believe about him; compose your own creed. Then pray your words with conviction.

FRIDAY OF THE FOURTH WEEK OF LENT

Like a shepherd he feeds his flock; in his arms he gathers the lambs, carrying them in his bosom, and leading the ewes with care. Isaiah 40:11

Church of the Ascension; Fountain Hills, Arizona

When I walk into this church hall, the first thing I notice on this plaster body of Christ is his arms. You can easily see the muscles and tendons outstretched, and I imagine that the artist wanted to show the humanity of Jesus—someone just like us. So what if Jesus had muscular arms instead of the long appendages that many crucifixion crosses show? He *was* just like me—my own muscular arms that I've proudly shaped through years of Zumba. I wonder: How did you get those muscles, Jesus? Before his public life, he was busy lifting wood and pounding nails—muscles fine tuned through honorable work. He was a craftsman who must have been proud of his creations and his hard work.

But when Jesus entered public life, all of that stopped. How did he keep his muscles in shape? He beckoned with those arms: "Come follow me." He gestured to the wide expanse of the crowd as he said to his disciples, "You feed them." When the woman caught in adultery stood accused before him, he doodled in the dust, biding his time before he told the crowd to throw the first stone if they had never sinned. Then he doodled some more while the crowd slipped away.

He stretched out his arms with a muscular power no man will ever know and calmed a storm at sea with his outstretched hands. This mighty feat filled the apostles with more terror than awe, for they recognized that it was more than muscular arms that had carried away the sea's tumult.

He outstretched his arms time and again to the broken, the paralyzed, the blind. And his last muscular effort before he hung on the cross with those arms was to carry a heavy piece of wood up the hill to Calvary.

He uses those arms to beckon me to follow. He feeds me with the arms that fed the multitudes. He helps me carry every heavy cross if only I lean on him and ask for help. His muscles will never fail me.

PRAYER

My Jesus, I feel the strength in your arms wrapped around me. You will never harm me with your power, and your arms hold me as tenderly as I once held my children when they were small. You are so strong and I am not. Your arms assure me that you are always with me. I will rest within your embrace, safe from the storm. Protected. Loved.

REFLECT & RESPOND

In all your interactions today, remember that Jesus is present and available to you—for guidance and for strength. Imagine him beckoning to you with his open arms. Go to him and ask specifically for what you need.

SATURDAY OF THE FOURTH WEEK
OF LENT

For I was hungry and you gave me food, I was thirsty and you gave me drink, a stranger and you welcomed me, naked and you clothed me, ill and you cared for me, in prison and you visited me." Matthew 25: 35-36

Chapel of the Milk Grotto; Bethlehem, Palestine

I first heard about the Chapel of the Milk Grotto in *Jesus: A Pilgrimage* by Fr. James Martin, SJ. A short distance from the Church of the Nativity, this chapel is devoted to Mary who supposedly nursed Jesus here before the Holy Family escaped to Egypt. The importance of the Blessed Mother is evident in this chapel, but I wasn't expecting to see this crucifix/statue high above the stairway leading down into the grotto. I quickly snapped this photo early in my 2019 pilgrimage, and it disappeared into my Holy Land album with all my other photos—until now during this Lenten season.

Jesus is bleeding from his head to his feet. His body is a mess, really. Yet St. Francis isn't afraid to enter into his mess and the chaos of the cross. At first I wasn't sure this was St. Francis of Assisi until I spotted the barely noticeable stigmata on the back of his hand. Another detail that may not be noticeable, especially because of how I had aimed my camera, is the left arm of Jesus resting on the shoulder of St. Francis. Obviously it was artistic license because nails had firmly anchored both arms of Jesus.

The loving embrace of St. Francis around the suffering body of Jesus reminds me of the story of St. Francis's encounter with a leper. Despite his fear and disgust of lepers, St. Francis got off his horse, kissed the leper, and gave him money. After St. Francis mounted his horse and looked back, the man had disappeared. St. Francis realized he had just kissed Jesus.

Like a leper, Jesus is scorned and rejected. You can almost hear St. Francis whispering, "I'm here, Lord," as he tenderly embraces Jesus's body. And Jesus is always ready to tenderly care for us as we endure our own suffering. Whenever you need to feel the presence of Jesus, imagine his arm resting on your shoulder, like he's doing here with St. Francis.

During Lent, we are called especially to reflect on the suffering of Jesus and to hear the call to be present to the suffering of others—to be like St. Francis was in this powerful crucifixion scene.

PRAYER

Lord, sometimes it is so hard to enter into the suffering of another—the mess, the chaos, the overwhelmingly helplessness of another, and to feel totally helpless myself. Be with me, Lord, when I want to turn away. Be with me, Jesus, when I want to run in the other direction. Give me the compassion that your servant Francis had for the poor and the suffering.

REFLECT & RESPOND

I believe we are called to be "God with skin" for others. Keeping this crucifix scene in mind, allow God to work through you today. Know that your presence matters. Choose to be deliberately present to someone in need of "God with skin."

FIFTH SUNDAY OF LENT

Amen, amen, I say to you, unless a grain of wheat falls to the ground and dies, it remains just a grain of wheat, but if it dies, it produces much fruit. John 12:20-33

Despite the Israelites breaking their covenant with God again and again, he doesn't turn his back on them. Jeremiah tells us that God places his law *within* his people and writes it upon their hearts. God says, "I will be their God, and they shall be my people." (Jeremiah 31:33) This new covenant, this new agreement between God and his people, includes you and me—and the reassurance that God won't turn his back on us even though at times we turn away from him. How can I not take a message like this to heart? How can a promise like this from God not reach the deepest part of me and somehow change my heart?

But wait, there's more, as the saying goes, as John's Gospel tells us. When this passage begins, some Greeks approach Philip and ask to see Jesus. Jesus then turns their request into a teachable moment about who he is and what it's like to follow him. It's not enough to just profess we love God. Jesus says, "Whoever serves me must follow me, and where I am, there also will my servant be." (John 12:26)

Being one of God's people like the first reading from Jeremiah describes is not enough either. We have to do more than just being claimed by God. We have to be like the grain of wheat that falls to the ground, dies in the darkness of the soil that it is planted in, sprouts new growth, and eventually produces much fruit. Following Jesus requires growth and transformation.

As Lent winds down these next two weeks, it's a great time to think about what I've been planting within my heart. How have I grown and been transformed? What will the fruit of this Lenten journey be?

> Jesus reveals that for every man and woman who wants to find him, He is the hidden seed ready to die in order to bear much fruit. As if to say: if you wish to know me, if you wish to understand me, look at the grain of wheat that dies in soil, that is, look at the **cross**.
> —Pope Francis, Homily, Fifth Sunday of Lent
> March 21, 2021

FIFTH WEEK OF LENT

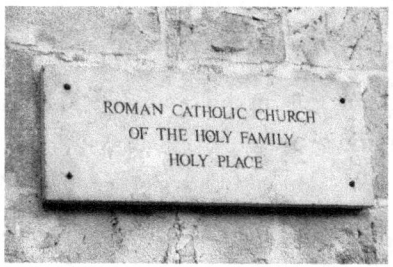

Anyone who's gone on pilgrimage, or even the tourist, knows how much more freely they travel who don't have a lot of baggage. The pilgrim knows that the small journey to a shrine, or to the holy places of one's religion, is a symbol of the journey home to God. The less baggage the better in order to remind the pilgrim of how little we take with us into eternity.

—Murray Bodo, OFM; *The Place We Call Home*

MONDAY OF THE FIFTH WEEK OF LENT

With loud shouts, however, they persisted in calling for his crucifixion, and their voices prevailed. Luke 23:23

St. Mary Catholic Church; Pella, Iowa

When I see this crucifix in a small Iowa town, I think: here's another enormous cross that completely overwhelms the body of Jesus. Just like the heavy crosses we bear. Like a devastating illness. Like a ruptured marriage. Like the death of a dearly loved daughter or son. Like the hatred and injustice that seem to have overtaken our country. How is hope possible under such a heavy weight?

Hatred and injustice sent Jesus to Calvary. But he accepted this suffering, and he bore it to the very end. Yes, he was God, but it was his human body that bled, cried out to God, and suffered an inhumane execution. Judas betrayed him, his disciples deserted him, and those who once hung on his every word eventually demanded that a murderer and insurrectionist be released instead of an innocent man.

The violence, injustice, and hatred I see every day in my newsfeed threaten to drain me of hope. When I read the account of the trial of Jesus, I see that the same kind of violence, injustice, and hatred existed when Jesus stood before Pilate. Why did the people hate this gentle man so much? I realize that the mocking taunts at political rallies today sound very much like the crowd shouting "crucify him."

There will always be suffering. There will always be evil. There will always be death. But there will always be the empty tomb and the triumph of the Resurrection. The love of Jesus overcame *everything*.

PRAYER

Lord, when grief and despair overtake me, don't let me fall under the weight. Lift me up and show me what is possible if I focus my eyes on your cross and choose to love like you, one person at a time.

REFLECT & RESPOND

We cannot save the world—Jesus already did that. When the suffering of the world seems too much to bear, remember to focus on loving one person at a time. This is actually a good practice even when you're not overwhelmed by what's going on in the world.

TUESDAY OF THE FIFTH WEEK OF LENT

Jesus said to him, "I am the way and the truth and the life. No one comes to the Father except through me. John 14:6

Church of the Beatitudes; Tiberias, Israel

In *Jesus: A Pilgrimage*, Fr. James Martin, SJ, talks about places in the Holy Land that were conducive for prayer and those that left him cold. This small chapel, however beautifully constructed, does nothing for me, probably because of the loud and sweaty tourists all around me who don't seem like they are on a holy pilgrimage.

Because of other pilgrims, I am barely able to gain a vantage point from which to photograph this stunning crucifix. Another photographer can be seen in the glass reflection, illustrating the life-size nature of this artist's portrayal of Jesus crucified. But the beautiful grounds outside the church and the view of the Sea of Galilee several feet below make more of an impression on me. On this mountain, Jesus cured many and fed the multitude of his followers.

After leaving the Mount of Beatitudes, we drive a short distance to Tabgha, the site near where the resurrected Jesus prepared a bread-and-fish breakfast for his disciples. Here on the shore of the Sea of Galilee, I am fed. I stop to breathe, to pray, to imagine Jesus standing exactly where I am standing. All the crucifixes, beautiful churches, and religious artwork had not been able to convey the presence of Jesus like I feel this day standing at the edge of the blue water where Jesus once walked over the waves. Here he called to his disciples; here he calls to me.

I bend over the clear water and gather several stones to bring home. The stones shine in the water like fine gemstones, but as they dried they look quite ordinary. Just like me. And in some ways, like Jesus looked as he walked this land doing extraordinary things—healing and teaching and bringing the dead to life. Yet his people couldn't accept the Messiah that he was. To them he must have looked like an ordinary stone on the shore of the Sea of Galilee—certainly not like anyone special. And like Pilate washing his hands of the blood of Jesus, the people in the crowd were probably thinking, "Well, that's that.

We got rid of this fake Messiah who stirs up people with his teaching."

Sometimes the voice of evil seems to prevail, but Jesus shows us that he is the way, the truth, and the life.

PRAYER

Today, Jesus, I remember those moments at the water's edge, the place where you called the first disciples. I thank you for calling me, for feeding me, for loving me, and for submitting your body to the cross. Help me to listen to your voice inside my heart so that I can discern what you would have me do for you.

REFLECT & RESPOND

Spend at least ten minutes today in silence reflecting on how Jesus is calling you. You may want to find a place in nature where you feel especially peaceful and are without distractions. Sometimes the voice of Jesus can be hard to hear.

WEDNESDAY OF THE FIFTH
WEEK OF LENT

I gave my back to those who beat me, my cheeks to those who plucked my beard; my face I did not shield from buffets and spitting. Isaiah 50:6

Roman Catholic Church of the Holy Family; The Old City, Jerusalem

During free time on my last afternoon of pilgrimage, I venture out with a few others to roam the Old City of Jerusalem. After visiting some shops, we come upon the Holy Family Hostel and decide to go inside to explore what the stone sign declares as "Roman Catholic Church of the Holy Family/Holy Place." Inside the hostel's cafeteria, we order delicious pastries. Although the dining room is inviting with its sunny windows, we carry our food outside to an intimate garden.

I leave the garden's sunshine to go inside for a restroom break and then decide to explore the hostel's main floor. At the end of the hallway, I stumble on a tiny chapel. So much is crammed into what is really a small room that I don't know where to look. Sanctuary lights and several elaborate coats-of-arms and lovely artwork and creaking wood pews—where to focus my attention? But there, right in the center of the altar and dwarfed by a large painting of the Holy Family, is a gold crucifix on top of the tabernacle with a golden door and the image of the risen Jesus. Sometimes it's easy to forget what is central to our faith.

On the wall outside the chapel is a painting of a crucifix that I did not photograph, but it somehow burned itself into memory. The artist portrayed the tortured face of Jesus, his body bleeding heavily from his knees. When you see something awful often enough—the bleeding hands, feet, and side of Jesus —it almost begins to lose its impact. But Jesus did fall three times on the way to his death. Maybe after he was arrested he also fell when the guards were pushing him around. This image of Jesus and his bleeding knees remind me of how much he suffered for me, in ways I hadn't even considered or couldn't even begin to fathom. How many skinned knees did I attend to and bandage when my children were growing up? Somehow I want to do the same for Jesus.

I carry home this simple yet powerful image of Jesus, tucked into my heart. For several months, I often remember those bloody knees, especially at Mass during the consecration as I hear, "This is my body."

PRAYER

Jesus, how can I ever take for granted what you did for me? How can I ever be blind to the blood you shed or be unaffected by your many bleeding wounds? Open my eyes, Lord. May I see and minister to the wounds of your people and thereby minister to you, Jesus.

REFLECT & RESPOND

Today be conscious of the walking wounded around you who conceal invisible wounds of pain or grief or loneliness. How can you provide some caring "first aid" to just one person today?

THURSDAY OF THE FIFTH WEEK
OF LENT

Then Mary said, "Behold, I am the handmaid of the Lord. May it be done to me according to your word." Then the angel departed from her. Luke 1:38

The Church of the Annunciation; Nazareth, North District, Israel

The Feast of the Annunciation, celebrated annually on March 25, usually occurs at some point during the Lenten season.

Revisiting the doors to this beautiful church in Nazareth seems fitting during this Lenten pilgrimage.

The same reason I love the San Damiano cross is the reason I love this door—both tell key stories of our faith. The stories on the left side of the door begin with the Annunciation and end with the shepherds in the field after the birth of Jesus. The stories on the right are a compressed look at the adult life of Jesus beginning with his baptism and ending with his Ascension into heaven. A prominent element of this door is the crucifix, along with Mary's presence at the foot of the cross.

An entry door is the perfect symbol for Mary. Jesus entered our world through the doorway of Mary's consent to be the Mother of God. She did not understand what awaited her on the other side of the door, but she trusted that this was *her* door and that God would be with her on the other side.

The crucifix too is an entry door. To the crowds gathered around watching the "spectacle" as Luke describes it (Luke 23:48), crucifixion was an exit and an ending. Who would have believed that the cross was the doorway to salvation and everlasting life?

So often I want certainty. I want to know if I should choose Door Number 1, 2, or 3 and which door will yield the best outcome. But I can make a wise and informed choice if I listen for the voice of God calling me to become the person he has in mind. For Mary, God called her to become the Mother of Jesus. And for Jesus, the Son of God, his mission was to become man and to do the will of his Father.

PRAYER

God, every day I am faced with choices and doors to open. Be with me as I discern my path each day. May I be like Mary and say "yes" to every door you place before me. Help me to rely on the guidance of the Holy Spirit to make wise choices. May I always trust, loving Father, that you desire what's best for me. Speak, Lord, your servant is listening.

REFLECT & RESPOND

Today make a conscious decision to be a doorway of God's love, and be especially kind to everyone you encounter.

FRIDAY OF THE FIFTH WEEK
OF LENT

"And just as Moses lifted up the serpent in the desert, so must the Son of Man be lifted up, so that everyone who believes in him may have eternal life." John 3:14-15

Creighton Retreat Center; Griswold, Iowa

I came upon this crucifix on the retreat center's wooded grounds during Joyce Rupp and Macrina Wiederkehr's Circle of Life retreat in 2017. Right here within this scene are signs of the life cycle—the green moss growing unchecked all over the crucifix and the leaves overhead beginning to change colors and loosen their hold on the trees.

Everything grows for a time. Everything changes. And then everything dies. But dying is never the end for us because of what happened on a blood-covered cross on which Jesus was lifted up.

Since that day on Calvary, people still suffer. Bones continue to get broken (just like the big toe of Jesus on this crucifix). Cancer and disease still cause suffering and death. Hatred still covers the earth like black mold. Yet we continue on, trying to follow the example of Jesus and to cover the earth with life-giving love, like a carpet of green moss. We cannot change the facts of the circle of life. But love can and will change everything.

PRAYER

God, I know that you make all things new. But sometimes it's hard to see newness in the middle of the darkness of suffering and death. I know that you are with me no matter what stage of the life cycle I'm in or where those that I accompany are in their life cycle. You alone hold our past, our present, and our future. Be with me, Lord, and help me to hang onto my hope in the promise of life everlasting with you.

REFLECT & RESPOND

Look around you today for someone who seems lonely or lost or sad. Cover them with your love, even if it's by offering only a small gesture of kindness. Be their source of hope today!

SATURDAY OF THE FIFTH WEEK OF LENT

"Behold, we are going up to Jerusalem, and the Son of Man will be handed over to the chief priests and the scribes, and they will condemn him to death." Matthew 20:18

Mount Tabor; North District, Israel

Today I reflect not on a crucifix but on the Jerusalem cross, an iconic Holy Land symbol, and the holy city it represents. Our pilgrimage tour guide informs us that this cross can be acquired only in Jerusalem, and not only is this symbol a popular item in the many tourist shops but it can also be found all over the city. This unusual cross, which did not originate until several centuries after the time of Christ, is the symbol of the city where Jesus died.

Jerusalem is the last stop of our pilgrimage that had been arranged according to the sequence of the life of Jesus. I vividly recall being on the tour bus, catching the first glimpse of the Holy City, and singing "Jerusalem, My Destiny" with fellow pilgrims. Like the arrival of Jesus in Jerusalem that we will commemorate tomorrow on Palm Sunday, our arrival is joyous and the capstone of our Holy Land journey.

Three times Jesus foretells his disciples what awaits him in Jerusalem. As they near the city, he tells them to make preparations for his triumphant yet humble entry into Jerusalem on the back of a donkey. The crowds who went ahead of him shouted their Hosannas, but after Jesus entered the city, Matthew tells us that the whole city was in turmoil and asking who this man was. Those following Jesus confirm that he is "the prophet Jesus from Nazareth in Galilee." (Matthew 21:10-11)

I wonder if Jesus experienced any inner turmoil before he enters Jerusalem and as he actually enters, knowing what he knew and anticipating what was to befall him. I think of people diagnosed with cancer or another devastating disease who, like my daughter, have the slimmest odds of survival but yet still hold onto hope. Jesus had no chance of surviving what would happen in Jerusalem. Still, he entered the city amid shouts of praise, and he didn't turn around and run the other way when the soldiers came to arrest him in the garden. If Jesus had been merely a man, surely our very human fight-or-flight response would have kicked in as soon as the soldiers approached to arrest him.

Yet because Jesus was a man who is also the Son of God, his mission was always to travel to Jerusalem, to remain there, and to submit to crucifixion, just as Isaiah had foretold: "like a lamb led to slaughter." Jerusalem was indeed his destiny—the place for both his death *and* his Resurrection.

PRAYER

My Jesus, be with me when I have to do really hard things that I would prefer not to do. Help me to rely on you and to lean on your rod and staff for courage. Whenever my fear threatens to overtake me, calm me with your loving presence like a guiding lamp. I do not see the road ahead, Jesus, but I know that you will be ever with me on my journey.

REFLECT & RESPOND

Tomorrow we will enter Jerusalem with Jesus as Holy Week begins. Spend some time thinking about what you'll do to make this last week of your Lenten journey with Jesus meaningful. Ask for the grace to accompany Jesus during this next week.

PALM SUNDAY

Then Jesus said to them, "All of you will have your faith shaken, for it is written: 'I will strike the shepherd, and the sheep will be dispersed.'"
Mark 14:27

Reading short scripture passages about the suffering and death of Jesus is hard enough; reading the entire Passion as we do on Palm Sunday is almost overwhelming. The thing I love about Mark's version is that, like me, he's into details. If we pay close enough attention to the details, it helps us enter the story and to imagine ourselves in the scene and even as one of the story's "characters."

Church of St. Peter in Gallicantu; Mount Zion, Jerusalem

But first I ask myself, who is Jesus? Other than Jesus responding "I am" to Pilate's initial questions, he speaks very little and does nothing to defend himself. He's not rebellious or cocky. He's gentle Jesus, an innocent man. He forgives his executioners. He forgives the good thief. As the bronze image of the imprisoned Jesus "Servus Domini" represents, the Servant of the Lord submits in obedience to the will of the Father out of love for you and me.

And who am I in this story?

✠ Am I the woman who spends a lot of money on a jar of ointment to anoint Jesus because I know *exactly* who he is?

✠ Am I one of the sleepy disciples in the Garden of Gethsemane who cannot stay present and awake to the suffering of Jesus?

✠ Am I one of the guards who beat, mocked, and spat at Jesus?

✠ Am I like Peter who denies knowing Jesus even after accompanying him for three years?

✛ Am I the maid who recognizes Peter and exposes his identity?

✛ Am I like Pilate who understands the innocence of the man before him, but cannot stand up to the crowd's demands?

✛ Am I like Simon of Cyrene who didn't volunteer to become involved in the crucifixion scene he stumbles onto but is pressed into service anyway?

✛ Am I the centurion standing at the foot of the cross who, upon witnessing Jesus take his last breath, knows immediately he was the Son of God?

A lot to contemplate this week.

PRAYER

Jesus, I want to stay by your side and accompany you on your journey to Calvary. But I am afraid that there are parts of me that are like so many of the people who were there the day you died—all of whom represent the light and the darkness in me. I believe that you are who you say you are, Jesus. Help me to accompany those who, like you on that day in Jerusalem, have no one to help them. Help me to be like the women who stayed with you until the end.

REFLECT & RESPOND

Today, take time on your own to slowly read Mark's account of the Passion (or Matthew's version), paying close attention to the details and the people that are included in the story of the final hours of Jesus. Which person are you most like? Which one are you least like? What do you notice about Jesus from this account of the Passion?

HOLY WEEK

Every significant journey changes us in some way. We are hardly ever aware of this while we are in the midst of it. We may have hints of these changes, but it is only later, in looking back, that we gasp in amazement at what was being formed and shaped in our lives. Only then do we recognize how a new attitude, a stronger dedication, and a fuller passion stretched us into the fullness of life.

—Joyce Rupp, *Walk in a Relaxed Manner*

MONDAY OF HOLY WEEK

When he returned to his disciples he found them asleep. He said to Peter, "So you could not keep watch with me for one hour?" Matthew 26:20

Nazareth, North District, Israel

Change is sometimes dramatic. Within a week's time, the weather here in Phoenix has gone from the 60s to the 90s. Kind of like the extreme change that happens in the week between Palm Sunday and Holy Saturday. Even as Jesus entered Jerusalem in triumph on Palm Sunday, the "heat" to put him to death was being generated by the chief priests and the elders.

Holy Week is filled with tension and drama and situations that change in a minute.

This last tumultuous week of Lent, I can choose to stand with Jesus. This crucifix behind the iron bars is a metaphor for my choice during Holy Week. The ironwork in this church is a separator, and it's difficult to determine much detail of the actual crucifix on the other side of it. Still, I can look through the wall of iron and ask what keeps me separated from Jesus.

Do I want to be a compassionate supporter or only minimally involved? Have I kept my heart behind bars and guarded it with a lock and key? Can I allow myself to imagine the pain of even one of the wounds that Jesus suffered?

A few days ago I heard someone on a podcast say that Lent is more about waking up than about giving up. Even as late as Holy Week, it's not too late to wake up to the radical and never-changing love of Jesus.

PRAYER

Dear Jesus, I'd like to think that I'd be the first to offer you loving support, to anoint your feet, or to lay down my cloak for you. I'd like to think that I would have stayed awake in the garden with you when you needed someone to be on standby and to pray. But I know that sometimes I have a wall of iron around my heart and I fail to do the most loving thing. Remove the iron bars, dear Lord, and make my heart more like yours.

REFLECT & RESPOND

Today ponder who or what you've closed your heart to. Take one small action step to unlock the bars of your heart. Ask Jesus for help if you find this a difficult task to do on your own.

TUESDAY OF HOLY WEEK

Jesus answered, "It is the one to whom I hand the morsel after I have dipped it." So he dipped the morsel and [took it and] handed it to Judas, son of Simon the Iscariot. John 13:26

St. Therese Catholic Church; Wrightsville Beach, North Carolina

Judas is on my mind today. Not because of any photograph but more likely because of this day's Gospel reading about the Last Supper when the "one whom Jesus loved" leans against Jesus's chest and asks who will betray him. Judas and the beloved disciple—two disciples whom Jesus chose, and two disciples who chose different paths.

Selling Jesus for thirty pieces of silver, the market price for a slave in those days, seems like such a heinous act. But before I judge what Judas did, I have to look at my own betrayals of Jesus, my own critical judgments of other people, my own acts of prideful behavior. Just today I found myself using very unkind words to describe someone—and then realized I really know very little about this person! A small betrayal perhaps, but a definite indication that I still have a long way to go toward my Lenten intention to be less judgmental.

But here in this photo is an example of faithfulness as the beloved disciple stands at the foot of the cross with Mary. He stood with her in her supreme moment of anguish and then took her into his home. He stood by his friend Jesus until the end. Staying power—that's what Jesus asks of us. Stay the course. Fall down and get back up. Decide to do better, to be better. Try to love like Jesus did. And don't judge people—even someone like Judas—because God's mercy is wider than we can ever fathom. His prodigal* mercy gives me—loved sinner that I am—hope.

*Note: Did you know that one of the definitions of *prodigal* is "lavish"? God is indeed a prodigal father who wants to extend his lavish love and mercy on each one of us! Does knowing this give you hope in God's wide and lavish mercy for you, even if you don't feel you deserve it?

PRAYER

Jesus, I so want to stay the course with you like your beloved disciple did. But often I fail to follow you as I should, even though I know you are the way, the truth, and the life. Help me to accompany you every step of the way as you walk to Calvary. Help me to persevere despite my own discouragement as I accompany friends who are sad, frustrated, or even feeling hopeless. Give me the grace of compassion and generous availability so that I can be like your faithful disciple who stood at the foot of your cross and stayed the course.

REFLECT & RESPOND

How willing are you to stay the course in accompanying someone who's ill or experiencing financial difficulty or is living in crushing grief? Ask for the grace of faithfulness like the beloved disciple and Mary model at the foot of the cross so that the next time you have an opportunity to accompany someone who is suffering, you will remain present to them and their needs.

WEDNESDAY OF HOLY WEEK

See, I am doing something new! Now it springs forth, do you not perceive it? In the wilderness I make a way, in the wasteland, rivers. Isaiah 43:19

St. Patrick Cathedral; Manhattan, New York

As Holy Week goes on, Jesus becomes increasingly alone, so this photo that I took in 2017 about ten weeks after my daughter's death seems appropriate. Jesus alone on the two crucifixes (one is so small you could miss it). The face of Jesus alone. Recalling the loneliness and isolation we all experienced during the pandemic, I am struck by how much Jesus suffered alone and was then cut off "from the land of the living" as Isaiah wrote (Isaiah 53:8).

The early stages of the pandemic reminded me of the grief and loss we experience after a loved one's passing—stifling and overwhelming feelings that go on and on without any promise of relief. Some of those feelings from the immense loss of a beloved never go away. I know that grief is eased by community and closeness, so I could not imagine how people in pandemic isolation coped with their grief when a loved one died. Public mourning was put on hold. But not grief.

The origin of the word *Lent* is "springtime." Is it any coincidence that this liturgical season occurs as the earth is waking up from winter and bursting into bloom?

Go spend some time in nature and allow it to teach you. Look around for signs of hope and emerging new life. Nature is trying to show you that grief and loss do eventually give way to a new normal. Inner growth is always possible from the dead places within. Transformation is always possible—slowly but surely. I just have to remember to trust in God's slow work as Pierre Teilhard de Chardin, SJ, reminds us in his prayer below.

PRAYER

Trust in the slow work of God. Your ideas mature gradually— let them grow, let them shape themselves, without undue haste. Don't try to force them on, as though you could be today what time (that is to say, grace and circumstances acting on your own good will) will make of you tomorrow. Only God could say what this new spirit gradually forming within you will be. Give Our Lord the benefit of believing that his hand is leading you, and accept the anxiety of feeling yourself in suspense and incomplete. Trust in the slow work of God. Amen.

REFLECT & RESPOND

How easy is it for you to trust in the slow work of God and feel yourself "in suspense and incomplete"? Today, ask for the grace of patient trust while God is bringing about something new within you.

HOLY THURSDAY

He advanced a little and fell prostrate in prayer, saying, "My Father, if it is possible, let this cup pass from me; yet, not as I will, but as you will." Matthew 26:39

The Church of All Nations, Mount of Olives/Garden of Gethsemane; Jerusalem

I try to imagine what Jesus may have felt that night in the garden by recalling those nights before a surgery or a medical procedure when I wrestled with worries, fears, and imagined thoughts about a future over which I had no control. Did Jesus grapple with similar feelings? I know he is God, but he was also a human being facing his death.

Recall a time you dreaded that something awful would happen. Do you remember being overtaken by fearful thoughts and your body's automatic response to the fear? If you are able to recall what it feels like to experience fear, anxiety, or even a panic attack, you may be able to imagine what Jesus may have experienced that night in the Garden of Gethsemane. He knew with absolute certainty that he would soon face a horrible death.

As Jesus experienced the physical signs of fear, sweat rolled off his head like drops of blood. (Luke 22:44) Yes, Jesus was spending his time in prayer, placing his trust in what his Father wanted. But like you and me in our humanity, he must have been overcome with fear of what was to come, a fear that Luke describes as "agony."

Approaching his sleeping disciples for the last time, Jesus must have heard the sounds of the approaching crowd. Did those sounds stop the churning of his anxious thoughts? Was it prayer that had calmed him so that he could courageously stand before the crowd and his betrayer?

Just inside the church next to the Garden of Gethsemane is this life-sized olive wood cross. In front of the altar is the large, flat stone said to be the one where Jesus prayed as he began his agony. The church and adjoining garden are located on a busy street outside the walls of the Old City.

A huge spotlight at the top of the church dimly illuminated the garden the night our pilgrimage group visited for a supposedly quiet hour of prayer. I realize now that the noises of the modern city outside the garden walls helped me to imagine the overwhelming, anxiety-ridden "sounds" that Jesus must have heard inside his head that night. Yet he still chose to follow the path set before him.

PRAYER

Jesus, in this dark garden you agonized over what was to come. Like your disciples, I cannot always focus on what you ask me to do. "Watch and pray" sounds like such a simple request, Lord. Help me to focus during those times when distractions overtake me, when I lose sight of what's really important. Ease my fears and worries when I cannot see the road ahead and uncertainty overtakes me. Illuminate my path with the spotlight of your love and do not allow fear to prevent me from making good choices. Be my ever faithful companion on this pilgrimage through life.

REFLECT & RESPOND

Recall an agonizing time where you once found yourself. Ponder how God was at work throughout this period of time. Were there any blessings that resulted from this time of suffering? Recall at least one of these in gratitude.

GOOD FRIDAY

Jesus gave a loud cry and breathed his last. Mark 15:37

While the original stone Stations of the Cross on the grounds of Franciscan Renewal Center were being restored, these simple signs marked the Way of the Cross for those praying the outdoor stations.

Often representations of the Stations of the Cross list only a Roman numeral without the station's title. Many stations attempt to realistically portray the scene so that we can imagine what it must have been like to be eyewitnesses of that day's events. My experience has been that the twelfth station, Jesus Dies on the Cross, usually includes those people present at the foot of the cross—Mary, other women, the beloved disciple, and even Roman guards.

However, on this Good Friday, this is what I see: the simple image of the San Damiano cross, the station's Roman numeral XII, and the five words describing the horrible and the terrible: Jesus dies on the cross.

His heart stopped beating.

He stopped breathing.

This Good Friday, April 2, 2021, marked the fourth anniversary of the day my daughter went home to heaven. Thinking of her last day in the hospital struggling for every breath made it all too easy for me to imagine Jesus having the same struggle during his last few hours. And then after one final breath, both of them were free from pain and so much suffering.

We never realize how precious a gift from God our very breath is, until each breath becomes a struggle. Or until we witness a loved one take their last breath.

PRAYER

Dear Lord, help me to value the gift of life in every breath you give me. May I never forget how you surrendered your life and your breath for me. Thank you, Jesus.

REFLECT & RESPOND

Spend some time on this solemn day to venerate the cross, either in your home or at a church. Do more than just gaze at it.

Let it touch your heart. Try to imagine that you are one of the bystanders, watching, waiting for Jesus to take his inevitable last breath.

If you are not good at imagining what it was like to stand at the foot of the cross, contemplate who Jesus is and what this means for you:

> It will do us good to look at the Crucifix in silence and see who our Lord is: he is the one who does not point a finger at someone, not even against those who are crucifying him, but opens his arms to all; who does not crush us with his glory, but lets himself be stripped for us; who does not love us in words, but gives us his life in silence; who does not force us, but frees us; who does not treat us as strangers, but takes our evil upon himself, takes our sins upon himself.
>
> —Pope Francis, Holy Week General Audience
> April 8, 2020

St. Margaret Mary Catholic Church; Omaha, Nebraska

HOLY SATURDAY

And Simeon blessed them and said to Mary his mother, "Behold, this child is destined for the fall and the rise of many in Israel, and to be a sign that will be contradicted—and you yourself a sword shall pierce—so that the thoughts of many hearts may be revealed." Luke 2:34-35

St. Mary of the Visitation Church; Iowa City, Iowa

Holy Saturday, such a liminal space. We wait for the Easter Vigil and the holy fire. We wait for Easter morning and the empty tomb. We wait for Resurrection.

After losing my child, I can all too easily imagine what it was like for Mary the day after her son died. She was not in the liminal space between death and life like those of us who know that Easter Sunday follows Good Friday. She wasn't waiting in anticipation of the next day when joy would return. Instead, I am certain that she spent this day overcome with raw grief, enduring her first full day of mourning. When I stand before this scene of Mary cradling the dead body of her son, I imagine what it was like for Mary the day after Good Friday, and this is what I write in my journal:

The events of the day before were seared into Mary's mind and her heart. At the foot of the cross she had watched as life drained from her son. She knew exactly what was going to happen; she knew her precious son would not live much longer. She witnessed each moment of his agony, and then it was mercifully over.

When they took down his battered body from the cross, she wanted her life to end too, so great was the pain. Pain that must have felt like the soul-piercing sword that the old man in the temple had predicted would befall her. She cradled her son's broken body and stroked his hair as she had done when he was a little boy. Gently she removed the crown of thorns from his bloody head and then helped Joseph of Arimathea and Nicodemus wrap his body in a linen cloth. She thought her heart would crack into two pieces when they rolled the stone in front of the tomb. John led her away and took her to his home.

She barely slept that first night as images of her son on the cross haunted her dreams and her sleepless moments in the darkness. The next day she arose as usual, but then in a flash she realized it was no longer a normalSabbath morning. Her son was gone. How could this be?

Throughout this Sabbath she rested restlessly while memories of yesterday's horror washed over her like a flood. Jesus had spoken a few times about being killed—although those close to him didn't believe this could ever happen—but he had also talked about being raised from the dead on the third day. And he **had** raised Lazarus on the fourth day. Dare she hope that his words were true? Would tomorrow be the day she would see her precious Jesus again? But suddenly her sorrow prevailed over her slim thread of hope, and her tears began—again.

PRAYER

Mary, be my model of courage and hope. Show me how to care for others as you cared for your son throughout his life, and mother me when my trials seem too much to bear. Help me to follow your example and be able to say, "Let it be with me according to your word."

REFLECT & RESPOND

Recall a time of uncertainty or darkness when you were unsure of the outcome. How did hope play a part? How does hope play a part in your life now? Thank God for the gift of hope.

EASTER SUNDAY OF THE RESURRECTION OF THE LORD

Then the angel said to the women in reply, "Do not be afraid! I know that you are seeking Jesus the crucified. He is not here, for he has been raised just as he said. Come and see the place where he lay." Matthew 28:1-8

"The Resurrection" bas relief; Our Lady of the Angels; Scottsdale, Arizona

He is risen! Shouldn't we all be shouting this Good News at the top of our lungs?

Resurrection is about the unexpected. It's about new life and the joy of new beginnings. It's about believing but not yet understanding. It's about hearing your name called by Jesus. It's about trying to hang on to his feet but being sent forth. Easter is about hope in the promise of the eternal life that awaits us after death.

What must it have been like to be Jesus waking up inside the complete darkness of the tomb? Did his heart suddenly begin to beat? Was he awakened from a deep sleep and had to reorient himself to where he was? One thing is for sure: We cannot fathom the miracle of Jesus being suddenly awakened from the sleep of death.

Still, I close my eyes for a moment to imagine what it must have been like to be Jesus that first Easter morning. The Gospel writers don't tell us what he experienced inside that dark tomb, but I imagine him waking with a start, opening his eyes, and taking a deep breath to fill his airless lungs. Did he realize what had just happened to him, or did he feel like I do sometimes when I wake up in the middle of a dream?

Suddenly, Jesus was himself again, outside the darkness of death, beyond the grave, raised to a new kind of life as both God and man, just as he had been all along, but now revealed in a whole new way in his resurrected body that still bore the wounds of what he had just been through. I like to think that when he fully realized all that had happened, he began to smile and became filled with a joy that we can only imagine. He himself was a miracle!

At some point, the angel who rolled away the stone announced to the women not to be afraid: Jesus had been raised, just as he had said. As the women hurried off to Galilee to announce this unbelievable yet joyous news, Jesus met them on the way. (Matthew 28:9-10) Like the women, we never know where we will encounter the Risen Lord.

This large bronze panel that depicts the Risen Jesus surrounded by post-Resurrection scenes has always held special meaning for me because it was installed into the outer wall of

Our Lady of the Angels Church the day of my daughter's funeral. Like the San Damiano cross inside the church, the bronze panel tells stories. These encounters with the Risen Jesus are **our** stories:

✛ Jesus feeds us like he fed the disciples breakfast on the shore.

✛ Jesus forgives us like he forgave Peter.

✛ Jesus welcomes us to experience his wounds like he asked Thomas to do.

✛ And Jesus continues to appear to us as the stranger on the road.

He is risen indeed!!

PRAYER

Sometimes in the face of so much discouragement and suffering, I forget what this incredible day represents. May I pause today to stand before the dark tombs in my own life and remember in awe and in joy that you, dear Jesus, overcame death and the darkness of your tomb. Thank you, Jesus, for inviting me to the new life that your Resurrection promises.

REFLECT & RESPOND

Look for signs of new life today. Slow down and observe something unexpected or surprising. Allow the joy of Easter to wash over you. **Rejoice!!**

TO GALILEE

THE PILGRIMAGE CONTINUES

Then Jesus said to them, "Do not be afraid. Go tell my brothers to go to Galilee, and there they will see me." Matthew 28:10

Sunrise over the Sea of Galilee

We live in Good Friday pain, Holy Saturday waiting, and Easter hope, all as interwoven as our lives.

—Kevin O'Brien, SJ; *Seeing with the Heart: A Guide to Navigating Life's Adventures*

MONDAY IN THE OCTAVE OF EASTER

Then they went away quickly from the tomb, fearful yet overjoyed, and ran to announce this to his disciples. And behold, Jesus met them on their way and greeted them. They approached, embraced his feet, and did him homage. Matthew 28: 8-9

St. Bernard of Clairvaux Catholic Church; Scottsdale, Arizona

I am not sure what it feels like to be fearful and overjoyed at the same time, but this is exactly what Matthew tells us Mary Magdalene and the other Mary felt as they ran away from the empty tomb to tell the disciples what they had seen. I imagine they experienced a tangled jumble of feelings, thoughts, and questions: Can this be? How can this be? Who took His body? Where is he now? When will we see him? What will he look like?

But before they'd gone too far, they saw Jesus and approached him. Can you imagine suddenly coming face-to-face with a loved one who has died? After the initial shock passed, I'd hug this beloved person tightly and cling to them like I'd never want to let go.

Upon seeing Jesus, the women's first reaction is to fall down on their knees and embrace his feet. I imagine them lovingly touching his open wounds, kissing his feet, and hanging onto those precious feet like they never want to let go. Jesus understands both their joy and their fear. He tells them not to be afraid, and he gives them a mission. What a surprising turn of events these two women experienced this Easter morning. What joy must have filled their hearts after they actually saw Jesus!

I picture the two running off joyfully yet occasionally stopping to turn around to see Jesus one more time. Then the two laugh and begin to dance, all along the road to Galilee. They are absolutely giddy with joy!

The message and mission that Jesus gave to the women is the same one he gives to you and me: Encounter the Risen Christ and be overjoyed. Tell others that you've encountered Jesus. Tell them to look for Jesus, too. Dance!

PRAYER

Jesus, today I ask for the grace to see the joy of the Resurrection everywhere I look. Help me to listen carefully to discern my mission and where you are sending me. May I share your joy with everyone I meet today.

REFLECT & RESPOND

Imagine the details of your reunion with a loved one who has died. Because of the Resurrection, we know that we **will** see them again! Allow your joy to lessen any sadness that you may feel when you remember this precious person.

TUESDAY IN THE OCTAVE OF EASTER

Jesus said to her, "Mary!" She turned and said to him in Hebrew, "Rabbouni," which means Teacher. Jesus said to her, "Stop holding on to me, for I have not yet ascended to the Father." But go to my brothers and tell them 'I am going to my Father and to your Father, to my God and to your God.'" John 20:16-17

Migdal, Israel; formerly Magdala, Mary Magdalene's birthplace

Today's reflection is an Ignatian Contemplation on this day's Scripture passage in which I imagine myself as Mary Magdalene at the empty tomb and her surprise encounter with the Risen Lord:

The body of Jesus is missing! Such surprise and confusion—on top of my crushing grief. The disciples have left me here in the garden, and I remain behind, to process the flood of my overwhelming feelings. I want to be alone to review in my mind all that has happened. To grieve. To feel my love for Jesus. To try to block out his suffering that I witnessed.

Tears fill my eyes, but then I am distracted as I hear someone nearby in the garden. I assume it's the gardener. I cannot really see him through my tear-soaked eyes, and all I see in the blinding morning sun is a man's silhouette. I tell him the version of the story I'm telling myself—that someone has stolen the body of my beloved Jesus! Just saying these words out loud renders me almost inconsolable. The man's response is to speak just one word: my name. I would know that voice anywhere, and my heart leaps as I again hear the voice of my friend, my beloved, **my** Jesus.

I embrace him, fall to my knees, and grab his feet as my tears of joy wash over his wounds. Jesus reaches down, takes my hand, and tells me to get up. He says I mustn't cling to him. He has a mission for me, and I'm to leave right away. "Yes, Jesus, I will do as you say!"

I turn and begin to walk away from him, but then a sudden impulse overtakes me. I run back to him and tightly embrace him. Jesus holds me gently, tenderly, as his head rests on top of mine. After a minute he whispers, "Now you must go." I release my iron grasp on him, laugh, and say, "Yes, Lord!" Off I run but every few feet I stop, turn around, and wave to Jesus. He smiles and waves back to me, Mary, his beloved friend.

The sound of Jesus saying Mary's name changes her day from a time of grieving into a day of gladness. Suddenly, her heart opens to something new and unexpected. She wants to linger with her beloved friend, but she responds in obedience to what he asks her to do. At that moment, she is the first and only one who knows Jesus is alive. Jesus chooses Mary Magdalene for a special mission, just as he has chosen each one of us to do something special.

PRAYER

Jesus, help me to hear you call my name and to respond in love. Today I ask for the grace to be surprised by joy. Open my eyes to your surprises everywhere and in everyone I meet today. Awaken me to the gladness of your Resurrection.

REFLECT & RESPOND

Think of someone who says your name in a special way, maybe when you greet them or when they are surprised to see you. Do they draw each syllable out or end the last syllable on an especially high tone? Perhaps they have a pet name that they alone call you. Although we cannot know what the voice of Jesus sounds like, we can imagine him saying our name in the same loving, surprised, and unique way like someone we know does. What do you do when you hear Jesus call you by name?

WEDNESDAY IN THE OCTAVE OF EASTER

And it happened that while they were conversing and debating, Jesus himself drew near and walked with them, but their eyes were prevented from recognizing him. Luke 24:15-16

The road to Emmaus from "The Resurrection" bas relief, Our Lady of the Angels; Scottsdale, Arizona

The Emmaus story is one of my favorite Scripture passages. There's mystery in the stranger who suddenly appears. There's the storytelling and the references to the ancient Scripture passages. And there's the light-bulb moment as Jesus breaks the bread. The two travelers immediately know that Jesus is in their midst just moments before he suddenly vanishes before their now-wide-open eyes. I imagine their joy when they decide to do an immediate U-turn and hightail it back to Jerusalem to report that they've seen the Lord. They felt joy at the very moment when they recognized Jesus breaking bread at the table. When they recalled their burning hearts as Jesus opened the Scriptures to them, they realized that their hearts had been burning and bursting with joy all along. And then, overflowing with joy, they carry this overwhelming news all the way back to their friends in Jerusalem.

The Emmaus story is the account of two different journeys these two disciples take. The first, when they are walking away from Jerusalem, is a journey of hopelessness and sorrow. It is a journey of heads hung low and hearts drooping. The second journey, representing the U-turn that these two take, is vastly different because they have encountered the Risen Christ—even if they did not recognize him at first. When the disciples beg Jesus to stay with them, he agrees—but only for a short time. Yet his brief appearance changes them, challenges them, sends them running off in joy to share the news that Jesus is indeed alive.

Every year, Easter is an invitation to undergo our own U-turns from sorrow and dejection to dancing joy. And as the poet Mary Oliver says, "Joy is not made to be a crumb."

PRAYER

Lord, I know that you use many things to try to grab my attention. But often my eyes are as clouded as the eyes of the two travelers on the Emmaus road. I read your Scriptures and I hear the testimony of holy men and women who have gone before me, yet sometimes it is hard to really see you, Jesus. Open my eyes and reveal yourself to me. Help me to respond without hesitation.

REFLECT & RESPOND

The two travelers did not sit around after they recognized Jesus. It was probably nightfall, but that didn't stop them from taking immediate action to return to Jerusalem to tell the disciples their news. Today, take action immediately when you think of something good that you could do or should do or intend to do . . . someday. Just do it right away!

THURSDAY IN THE OCTAVE OF EASTER

While they were still speaking about this, he stood in their midst and said to them, "Peace be with you." But they were startled and terrified and thought that they were seeing a ghost. Luke 24:36-37

Segovia Cathedral; Segovia, Spain

As the scripture passage from Luke opens, the disciples are listening to the surprising news report of the two Emmaus disciples. Eyewitness reports or not, how were the disciples supposed to believe this story that Jesus was alive? And then suddenly in their midst, there he stands—poof, like a ghost! After he shows them his hands and his feet, their fear and disbelief turn to joy and amazement. Jesus is really and truly present!

The only way we can possibly understand all that the disciples experienced that day is to imagine a similar scene taking place in our own homes. A family member who recently died suddenly appears and begins talking to you. What are your first thoughts? Do you think that maybe your grief has you seeing things? What does it take for you to finally believe that this "ghost" is really real and your family member has truly returned?

Place yourself in the room with the disciples that first Easter Sunday. What does it look like for you to be "incredulous for joy" while also being amazed? Now, imagine yourself receiving the peace, healing, and mercy that the Risen Jesus offered to his disciples when he returned to them.

Peace. Healing. Mercy. This is what it means to live our lives like we are Easter people! Truly we are called to live as pilgrims of hope!

PRAYER

Dear Jesus, I want to be your follower. I want to believe everything I've read about you in Scripture. Sometimes it's hard to let go of my need to understand the mystery surrounding your Resurrection. Strengthen my faith and trust in you. Heal my doubts by your mercy. Fill me with your peace, Jesus.

REFLECT & RESPOND

"Peace be with you." For ten minutes, sit in silence as you breathe in the peace of Jesus and breathe it out to our wounded world. As you leave this time of silence, make an intention to carry the peace of Jesus with you into your day.

FRIDAY IN THE OCTAVE OF EASTER

Jesus said to them, "Come, have breakfast." And none of the disciples dared to ask him, "Who are you?" because they realized it was the Lord. John 21:12

Jesus and the disciples from "The Resurrection" bas relief at Our Lady of the Angels; Scottsdale, Arizona

Can you imagine the disciples' joy that morning when they realized it was the Lord waiting for them on the shore? Whether this was the first time they saw him or the fourth, it still must have been both joyous and a little confusing, especially since they didn't recognize him right away.

I wonder what Jesus looked like that day as stood on the

shore yelling out to them in the boat, referring to them as "children," and instructing them where to drop their nets. Was he filmy and flowy like I sometimes imagine him? Was his face concealed so that the disciples couldn't clearly see him until they got closer to him on the shore? And what would it feel like to have Jesus cook breakfast and invite me to come eat with him?

The disciples truly weren't expecting to find Jesus on the shore that day. Is it possible Jesus makes unexpected "appearances" in our lives today? A principle of Ignatian spirituality is to find God in all things. This also means to find God in all *people*. How do we know that Jesus isn't still walking among us and that we can see him "in the least of these"? But only if we dare to come closer.

Perhaps Jesus makes random appearances in different disguises like St. Teresa of Calcutta used to say—seeing the presence of Jesus in his "distressing disguises."

As my dad used to tell me when I was little, "Keep your eyes peeled!"

PRAYER

Draw me to you, Jesus. Feed me every day with your breakfast of everlasting love, mercy, and compassion. Let me see your face in those who are suffering—the lonely, the hungry, the homeless. Then help me to feed them with the same abundance of love you've lavished on me.

REFLECT & RESPOND

Choose one meal today to eat mindfully and gratefully. Be conscious of the many pairs of hands that labored so that you could eat the meal before you. Be appreciative of the farmers, the harvesters, the truckers, the grocers, and lastly, the one who prepared this food on the plate in front of you. Contemplate the interconnected web that we all are part of. Give thanks as you chew each bite.

SATURDAY IN THE OCTAVE OF EASTER

She [Mary Magdalene] went and told his companions who were mourning and weeping. When they heard that he was alive and had been seen by her, they did not believe. Mark 16:10-11

St. Louise Catholic Church; Bellevue, Washington

Mark's version of the encounter with the Risen Christ that Mary Magdalene and the disciples on the road to Emmaus experience is bare bones compared to Luke's version. In five short verses, Mark provides brief facts about the appearance of

Jesus to Mary Magdalene, her sharing of the news with his mourning and weeping "companions," their doubting disbelief, and his appearance to the two "walking along their way to the country." Talk about the Cliffs Notes version of what happened on that first Easter Sunday!

Perhaps Mark left out many details so that we could picture ourselves in this story: We in our times of mourning and weeping. We in our moments of disbelief. And we who often wander along the way while running away from an unexplainable, heart-breaking event.

In his homily on Easter Sunday April 4, 2021, Pope Francis said:

> From the rubble of our hearts, God can create a work of art; from the ruined remnants of our humanity, God can prepare a new history. He never ceases to go ahead of us: in the cross of suffering, desolation and death, and in the glory of a life that rises again, a history that changes, a hope that is reborn.

What does it take for you and me to believe in hope reborn?

PRAYER

Risen Lord, I ask that hope be reborn in me this day. Take away my sadness and despair for our hurting world. May I have faith that you can indeed create a new future. May I be a willing participant in your creation of a new work of art—one that is painted with the broad strokes of love and compassion. May you always walk with me, near me, and ahead of me.

REFLECT & RESPOND

For just one day, let go of your expectations of how you imagine things are going to go—how they historically go—and leave room for God's grace to create something new and unexpected. Imagine some of these new possibilities and dreams that God may have for you that you never even dare to consider. Ask for the grace to believe that all things are possible with God.

SECOND SUNDAY OF EASTER
(SUNDAY OF DIVINE MERCY)

Then he said to Thomas, "Put your finger here and see my hands, and bring your hand and put it into my side, and do not be unbelieving but believe." John 20:19-31

Thomas & Jesus from "The Resurrection" bas relief; Our Lady of the Angels; Scottsdale, Arizona

Thomas the apostle rightfully earned his "Doubting Thomas" name by refusing to believe that Jesus had risen and appeared to the other disciples. It is surprising that Thomas doubted *eyewit-*

ness accounts. These were his close friends! Didn't he trust them? Or was he the kind of person who just had to see it with his own eyes?

So what did Thomas do when Jesus appeared to the disciples a week later and urged Thomas to touch his wounds? I imagine Thomas was humbled, perhaps overcome with embarrassment and shame. Did he fall to his knees? Did he touch even one of the wounds that Jesus was holding out to him? Actually, the passage doesn't say what he actually did. We are simply told that Thomas exclaimed the often-repeated words of praise, "My Lord, and my God!"

In his Easter message of April 4, 2021, Pope Francis observes: "When Thomas sees the wounds of Jesus, his own wounds of pride and shame and doubt are healed." Yes, seeing the wounds of Jesus was healing for Thomas, but the reaction of Jesus—or what Jesus did not do—is what completed this healing. When Thomas stood before him, Jesus could have reprimanded Thomas, ridiculed him, or embarrassed him for failing to believe his friends. But Jesus was gentle, inviting, telling Thomas to do what he needed to do to believe. Jesus then says to Thomas (also to us non-eyewitnesses) that those who believe without seeing are blessed.

That day, Jesus accepts who Thomas is—and he simply loves him and offers him tender mercy—just as Jesus does with us when we question and doubt. Like he did with Thomas, Jesus offers us mercy after mercy after mercy.

I like to think that on that Sunday, Thomas gained the bold confidence to be who he was—loved by Jesus, no matter what. Later, after Jesus told the apostles to go and make disciples of all nations, they all took this mission seriously. (Matthew 28:19) Yet it is believed that Thomas journeyed the farthest (to India!) spreading the Good News.

Like Thomas, we are sent on a journey to be "Pilgrims of Hope," the theme Pope Francis chose for the 2025 Jubilee Year.

If we travel our pilgrimage of life with hope, St. Paul assures us that "hope does not disappoint." (Romans 5:5) Hope is the walking stick we can lean on when the journey becomes difficult and our steps falter.

And so, my fellow pilgrim, we end our sacred journey together where we began: focused on the wounds of Jesus. We celebrate that his wounds have freed us, and we believe without seeing that our own wounds can and will be healed through him. Let us continue on our earthly pilgrimage, ever mindful that Jesus always accompanies us. He is our ever-present companion, our strength, and our hope.

PRAYER

Help my unbelief, Lord, when I cannot see you walking beside me in my everyday life. Help my doubt when I cannot see how much you love me. By your mercy, restore me so that I may trust and hope in you. By your wounds, heal me, Jesus. Make me whole.

REFLECT & RESPOND

In her poem "The Wren from North Carolina," Mary Oliver writes of observing a wren singing "a line of grace notes I couldn't even write down." She describes the wren having a small cup of life "that he drinks from every day" before delivering a song of praise. She points out that she too has "her morning cup of gladness."

To give us plenty of practice living like Easter people, the season of Easter lasts fifty days. During the rest of these fifty days, make it a daily practice to look for your own morning cup of gladness. You don't necessarily have to find this daily dose of joy in the morning; it can be any moment of the day when you feel the warmth of joy spreading inside your heart.

The more you watch for these moments, the easier it will be to see them. If you keep a journal, describe what you see. Then at night, reflect back in gratitude on this daily moment of gladness.

As the poet Mary Oliver says, "Sometimes I need only to stand wherever I am to be blessed."

EPILOGUE

Creighton Retreat Center; Griswold, Iowa

OCTOBER 29, 2017

I sit in front of the stone of grief in the tomb of sorrow. I'm trying to believe in your Resurrection, Lord. Yes, Lord, I do believe but sometimes, sometimes it just doesn't seem right or fair. Your resurrected golden arms reach out to me. They say,

"Peace be with you." As the leaves drop one by one, gently floating to the earth, to death, then to rebirth, I imagine my daughter's beautiful spirit as it floated to you, from death to new life. Everything passes and changes. Even you, Jesus, from death to life and then to heavenly life. As will I.

Dry my tears and let me use this sorrow—this horrible, bad grief—for good. That's what my sweet daughter would want. She would be sad that I am sad. I imagine what she would say to me: *I'm okay, Mom, I really am. And I want you to be okay, too. Know that the waves of sadness will come and go—crashing and receding. Heaven really is a better place, Mom. And one day I'll see you here. Until then, live gratefully and be kind.*

Thank you, God, for my daughter's life—every precious minute of it. Help me to remember its sweetness and not its sorrow. Help me to grow from this and to use it to help and to heal others. Allow my prayer to make me an instrument for your peace. For your kingdom. For your people. For you.

Thank you for the gift of life surrounding me—the tapping woodpeckers and the chortling bird song. Thank you for the clouds and the canopy of trees. Thank you for autumn's many signals of approaching winter. Thank you for this glorious fall day that is teaching me what I need to learn and what I need to let go of. Thank you for helping me be present to all that is.

OCTOBER 4, 2021

On the feast of St. Francis, I set out on a mini-pilgrimage to revisit Creighton's retreat center in rural Iowa. I especially wanted to see the very visual image of the large "stone of grief" behind the Risen Jesus where my grief had come spilling out four years ago. Today the retreat center is nearly deserted, and I sit with my journal in the forest surrounded by birds singing and woodpeckers knocking and squirrels chattering. The bench where I rest looks new, but the Resurrection statue is not–it's the same as it was four years ago when I wept before it, my eyes blurred with grief.

What message do you have for me today, Jesus? Your arms are still wide open, but your eyes no longer appear to be cast downward like they seemed the last time I was here. For a minute I wonder if this really *is* the same statue. Perhaps the sunshine makes the statue look different? But more likely, it's because—by your grace, Lord—I am not the same person I was four years ago. Now your eyes look outward at me seated before you, as I am in awe and in absolute amazement. You rose, Jesus! That promise is for me as well. For my sweet daughter. For all of us. I believe your very Word when you promised: "I am the resurrection and the life; whoever believes in me, even if he dies, will live." (John 11:25)

Thank you, Jesus, for loving me as wide as your arms reach–even wider than your arms reach! As wide as your heart of boundless love and compassion.

ONE LAST AND LASTING PRAYER

Jesus, I have followed you on this pilgrimage of your holy cross
to your empty tomb.
I have followed you
on the path of suffering and death to joy.
Be my strength and my rock on this continuing earthly
pilgrimage whenever my feet fail to follow you
or when I find it hard to love like you do.
Season after season, help me to learn to accept
things as they are:
the unfolding and the folding,
the beginnings and the endings.
Help me to feel your presence in every situation I encounter—
whether I like what's happening or not.
Be with me this day and always.
Jesus, I place my hope in you.

THREE PRAYER PRACTICES

VISIO DIVINA, LECTIO DIVINA, AND IGNATIAN CONTEMPLATION

I. VISIO DIVINA

This prayer practice encounters God through images.

Visio Divina, Latin for "divine seeing," invites you to engage deeply with an image in a contemplative manner. Rather than merely observing an image, you allow yourself to be immersed in it, seeking spiritual insights, connections, and revelations. The practice of Visio Divina is similar to Lectio Divina, the second prayer practice described, in which you meditate on sacred texts.

The Five Steps of Visio Divina are as follows:

1. Prepare: Choose an image that resonates with you. It could be a painting, photograph, or any visual representation that draws you in.

2. Gaze: Look at the image quietly, allowing your eyes to roam and take in the details. Notice colors, shapes, textures, and emotions that arise.

3. Reflect: What captures your attention? What emotions or thoughts surface as you gaze at the image? What spiritual themes or messages emerge?

4. **Pray:** Engage in a conversation with God. Offer gratitude, seek guidance, or express the feelings that the image evokes within you.

5. **Contemplate:** Sit in silence, allowing the experience to settle within you. Let the insights you gained resonate deeply.

INCORPORATING VISIO DIVINA INTO DAILY LIFE

You don't need a monastery or special training to practice Visio Divina. Simple practices, such as observing nature, appreciating artwork, or even contemplating photographs such as the ones in this book, can be woven into your daily routine and serve as a gentle reminder in our fast-paced lives to pause, reflect, and seek God in the ordinary.

Visio Divina invites us to quiet our minds, open our hearts, and discover the profound beauty and wisdom that reside in the simplest of images.

II. LECTIO DIVINA

This prayer practice encounters God through Scripture.

Lectio Divina, or "sacred reading," is an ancient practice from the Christian tradition, dating from the early medieval era of prayerful study of Scripture in monasteries. Lectio Divina is a slow, quiet, and thoughtful practice to encounter God through Scripture. Reading, rereading, and responding to a a passage of Scripture provides time and space for God's Word to move from your lips, into your mind, and finally into your heart.

This prayer practice is also a listening practice, and the word "listen" is based on the root word for "obey." In this practice, you listen more deeply to Scripture than you would likely do during a liturgy, and then you contemplate how God is speaking to you and what he is inviting you to do.

It's an unhurried practice and requires you to engage with your heart and your imagination. Basically, you focus on the questions of: What is the text saying to me? What does the text say about who God is? How is God moving in my life and in the world?

Although the steps of this prayer practice are based on Latin words, these steps are simply Read, Meditate, Pray, and Contemplate.

1. **Read.** Focus on becoming familiar with the text by reading it slowly. If there are there any words you don't understand, look them up. Slowly read the passage again, noticing any words or phrases that seem to jump out at you or attract your attention.

2. **Meditate.** Reflect on the passage and especially on what grabbed your attention or attracted you.

3. **Pray.** Read the passage a third time and consider what God is saying to you. What feelings are arising within you? What are you wondering about? Talk to God about the words

or an image you are drawn to. What is God inviting you to think about or calling you to do? Prayerfully consider the gentle invitation from God that is often hidden in that which captured your attention.

4. **Contemplate.** Read the passage a final time. Then be still and rest in the presence of God.

III. IGNATIAN CONTEMPLATION

This prayer practice uses the imagination to encounter Jesus in Scripture.

Ignatian Contemplation is a method of prayer developed by St. Ignatius of Loyola, the founder of the Jesuits. It is a form of imaginative prayer that involves using your imagination to enter into a Gospel scene, experiencing it as if you're actually there, and engaging with it fully.

1. **Select a Scripture passage from the Gospels** that involves a story. Read it twice, slowly.

2. **Engage your imagination and place yourself in the scene**. Use your senses to visualize the scene, creating it in your mind by seeing, hearing, smelling, and tasting what it is like to be present in that moment. Don't be afraid to lose yourself in the story and don't worry if your imagination is running a little too wild. Trust that God is trying to communicate with you through this prayer practice.

3. **Engage with the scene.** You might be a bystander, a participant, or even one of the central "characters." Imagine yourself interacting with the characters, including Jesus. Observe the reactions and responses of those in the scene with you.

Some people may find it difficult to imagine the scene. However, observing your feelings and emotions is another way to experience the scene. For example, you might find yourself feeling the shame of the woman caught in adultery as she is brought before Jesus. Or you may feel the joy of the parents after Jesus brings their daughter back to life. Feeling compassion for the people that Jesus encounters may be another response.

You may also choose to write down what comes to you

during this experience like some of the reflections that are included in this book. Pray the way that is best for you!

4. **Reflect** on what happened while you were creating this scene in your imagination. What did you feel? What stood out to you? What may God be trying to communicate with you through this imaginative prayer?

5. **Converse with Jesus** about this experience and share what's in your heart. The purpose of Ignatian Contemplation is to draw closer to Jesus. You may find that you understand what's going on in your own life as a result of this new way of being with Jesus.

An excellent resource for practicing Ignatian Contemplation can be found in *Learning to Pray: A Guide for Everyone* by Fr. James Martin, SJ. Within this comprehensive book, Fr. Jim devotes an entire chapter on "The Gift of the Imagination." Here's one piece of advice from this chapter, and the first and last sentences are a good summary of all three prayer practices:

> As in any prayer, allow God to lead you. In the Nativity, if you are drawn to spend time quietly contemplating the scene and feeling a spirit of peace, that's fine. If you are moved to something more specific, that's fine too. Trust that God is leading you and will raise up what you are meant to look at.

FOR FURTHER EXPLORATION

The following resources are listed in order of their reference within this book:

Paintner, Christine Valters. *The Soul of a Pilgrim: Eight Practices for the Journey Within*. Notre Dame, Indiana: Sorin Books, 2015.

Martin, James, SJ. *Jesus: A Pilgrimage*. New York: HarperOne, 2014.

Boyle, Gregory, SJ. *Tattoos on the Heart: The Power of Boundless Compassion*. New York: Free Press, 2010.

Ignatian Spirituality website: https://www.ignatianspirituality.com/pilgrimage-2

What is Ignatian Spirituality: https://www.ignatianspirituality.com/what-is-ignatian-spirituality/

Examen with James Martin, SJ : https://podcasts.apple.com/us/podcast/the-examen-with-fr-james-martin-sj/id1346804716

Martin, James, SJ. *The Jesuit Guide to (Almost) Everything: A Spirituality for Real Life*. New York: HarperOne, 2010.

Doyle, Brian. *Eight Whopping Lies and Other Stories of Bruised Grace*. Cincinnati: Franciscan Media, 2017.

Wiederkehr, Macrina, OSB. *Seasons of Your Heart: Prayers and Reflections*. New York: Harper Collins, 1991.

Bodo, Murray, OFM. *The Place We Call Home: Spiritual Pilgrimage as a Path to God*. Brewster, MA: Paraclete Press, 2004.

Rupp, Joyce. *Walk in a Relaxed Manner: Life Lessons from the Camino*. Maryknoll, New York: Orbis Books, 2005.

O'Brien, Kevin, SJ. *Seeing with the Heart: A Guide to Navigating Life's Adventures*. Chicago: Loyola Press, 2023.

Martin, James, SJ. *Learning to Pray: A Guide for Everyone*. New York: HarperOne, 2021.

Oliver, Mary. *Why I Wake Early*. Boston: Beacon Press, 2004.

Oliver, Mary. *Devotions: The Selected Poems of Mary Oliver*. New York: Penguin Press, 2017.

Homilies of Pope Francis by topic https://www.popefrancishomilies.com/home

WITH GRATITUDE

Gratitude is one of the pillars of Ignatian Spirituality, so first I want to acknowledge a Jesuit I've never met, Fr. James Martin, SJ, whose book *Jesus: A Pilgrimage* has greatly influenced me. I am grateful he wrote a book that helped me see Jesus in a new light as well as kindling my interest in pilgrimage.

I am also grateful to the Jesuits Midwest Province and their yearly "pilgrimage" to Phoenix to present Lenten Mornings of Reflection where I was first introduced to Ignatian Spirituality in 2009. Although I wholeheartedly embraced this spirituality, I never felt fully Ignatian before I did the Spiritual Exercises of St. Ignatius. During the pandemic, doing the Exercises became possible when Santa Clara University and an amazing team assembled an online version of the Nineteenth Annotation, the Spiritual Exercises in daily life.

The San Damiano cross has played an important role in my life from the time I began worshipping at the Franciscan Renewal Center, the "Casa." My appreciation goes to Fr. Vincent Nguyen, OFM, whose beautiful icon of the San Damiano cross hanging high above the altar of the Church of Our Lady of the Angels stirs my heart every time I gaze at it.

Putting together a book has been a labor of love. I'm grateful for the support and encouragement of my daughters Kate, Kari, and Kimberly. And kudos to Kari for her beautiful cover design! Thanks also goes to my husband, Bernie, who assured me that if even one person is moved by this book, my investment in self-publishing would be worth it. Special thanks to my editors,

Debi Wiskirchen and Tom Sparough, for their helpful edits and guidance.

I'm especially grateful to Brenda Phillips who asked me to write Lenten reflections for her. Left to my own devices, I'd still be talking about writing these "someday." I'm grateful for the directees and friends who read and affirmed early versions of these reflections, formerly known as my "crucifix project." Thank you to my two writing buddies, Deb Findlow and Cathy Gomez, for their encouragement and wisdom. Every woman needs a BFF cheering her on, and I'm thankful that Jennifer Fabiano is mine.

Finally, I have been blessed with wonderful spiritual support: my Ignatian spiritual director, Lynne Lukenbill; and my Franciscan support team: Fr. Page Polk, OFM; Fr. Vincent Nguyen, OFM; Fr. James Seiffert, OFM; and Deacon Matt Ryan, OFM. I'm also blessed by the influence of my friend across the pond, Fr. Simon O'Connor, whose poetic vision and wise perspective have enriched my faith.

Most all, I'm grateful to our great God who placed this desire in my heart to follow Jesus and his cross all the way to Jerusalem and Calvary and then to share this pilgrimage with others.

AMDG: For the Greater Glory of God!

ABOUT THE AUTHOR

Diane Amento Owens is a spiritual director, a freelance editor and writer, and the mother of four grown and flown daughters (including Kali who flew home to God's arms on April 2, 2017). To honor her Sicilian father and grandfather whose writing genes she inherited, Diane includes her maiden name "Amento" in her writing name. A cradle Catholic, she now worships at a Franciscan church/retreat center where she serves as a spiritual director, proclaims the Word, livestreams daily Mass for the homebound, and is on the OCIA team. Her spiritual life was enriched the day she learned about Ignatian Spirituality at her first Jesuit Morning of Reflection, and she's since written reflections for Jesuit Prayer, a daily prayer app. Shortly after Kali's death, Diane chose to learn and grow from the most horrible thing that ever happened to her, and she decided to live a life of purpose by helping others. This book is the fruit of that desire. You can find more of Diane's photography and writing at https://dianeowens.com/